SCOTLAND'S JESUS

D0988167

★ THE ONLY OFFICIALLY ★
NON-RACIST COMEDIAN

FRANKIE BOYLE

SCOTLAND'S JESUS

HARPER

Northamptonshire Libraries & Information Services	
Askews & Holts	

1 3 5 7 9 10 8 6 4 2

© Frankie Boyle 2013

Frankie Boyle asserts the moral right to be
identified as the author of this work

This book contains material previously published elsewhere,
including in Frankie Boyle's *Sun* columns

A catalogue record of this book is
available from the British Library

ISBN 978-0-00-742684-3

Printed and bound in Great Britain by
Clays Ltd, St Ives plc

All rights reserved. No part of this publication may be
reproduced, stored in a retrieval system, or transmitted,
in any form or by any means, electronic, mechanical,
photocopying, recording or otherwise, without the prior
written permission of the publishers.

MIX
Paper from
responsible sources
FSC C007454

FSC™ is a non-profit international organisation established to
promote the responsible management of the world's forests.
Products carrying the FSC label are independently certified to
assure consumers that they come from forests that are managed
to meet the social, economic and ecological needs of present
and future generations, and other controlled sources.

Find out more about HarperCollins and the environment at
www.harpercollins.co.uk/green

CONTENTS

INTRODUCTION

There are many reasons why an author chooses to write a book. Perhaps, like me, they're being paid a lot of money to write it. Or perhaps . . . nope, that's all I can think of. The good people at HarperCollins did gently hint that I should make this book more commercial, so I had to ask myself about the nature of what's popular in our culture. What do people really want? What would we hope to be offered by a book if we were being completely honest? Which is why I started writing the book you now hold in your hands. A crime porno.

The appeal for me was simple. How hard can it be to write a thousand words of porn every day? *I probably text a thousand words of porn a day*. The real problem was not *only* writing porn and letting the whole thing descend into a kaleidoscope of mouths and limbs and cocks and mouths and cocks. Cocks. And tits.

Hence crime. I've never met anyone who doesn't like a little vicarious contact with crime: from teenagers killing prostitutes in *Grand Theft Auto* as a bit of light-hearted escapism from their actual sex lives, to the talcum-powder market foaming their knickers at *Daily Mail* headlines. The appeal is complex but, for whatever reason, it excites us to hear about some cunt getting killed.

My teenage sexual awakening happened long before the internet. I used to hang out at my local library and scour thrillers for sex. I'd skim the sort of doorstoppers you'd find on your uncle's bookshelf for words like 'grasped' and 'thrust'. Occasionally looking up to stare slack mouthed at real women trying to borrow books, I rejected the opportunity for precocious learning and memorised reams of disjointed encounters between guilt-ridden adulterers, mercenaries and whores, and even the desperate couplings of a Southern slave plantation. Perhaps this has affected my adult life. I've spent this speeding disinterestedly through the bits central to the narrative, desperately looking forward to the occasional sexual episodes, which I haven't fully understood.

So part of me imagines this book hitting the Scottish library system, and some wee Wifi-less schoolboy in Penicuik having his aching balls blown off by this filthy lightning bolt of premeditated degradation. Or some guy getting his teenage daughter it as a present, because he remembers me from *Mock of the Week*. Merry Christmas, love!

This will be the burning bible of teenage Britain; a suppressed memory; a limping man in a wooden mask announcing with a shriek that he is the only guest of your surprise birthday party; an uncomfortable evening at the launch of a Muslim breakfast cereal; walking into a bar where a pub quiz host's questions about your private life are met with general laughter and the harsh metallic bleat of a deer; a sore arse;

your dog returning home with a swear word shaved into its side. This book will replicate almost exactly the experience of being a guy who gets raped just after getting the all-clear from prostate cancer and, as the rapist says how tight he is, he realises the cancer's back; it will be a jeering portal into a new dimension of Desperate Iniquity.

Well, I suppose, to be entirely accurate, I sent HarperCollins the outline of a crime porno and they told me to fuck off. Instead, they asked me to produce what you hold in your hands. I was asked to deliver a humorous topical Christmas book, the sort of thing that raises a wry eyebrow at the news. A Jeremy Clarkson-style slab of bouncy opinion that, with the right cover, might sell well in train stations.

However, they did say that the introduction wasn't too important and I could maybe let loose a little there. Most people skip the introduction, and half the people who get a book in a train station never read the fucking thing. So for the rest of the introduction I want you to imagine that you're reading a crime novel. A crime novel in which many of the leads the investigator pursues seem to end in almost pointlessly graphic sex scenes.

• • •

The taxi pulls up by a little boxy end of terrace. After this, it's all just countryside; after the street lamp on the corner, there's nothing. I pay the cabbie and get out with her. She turns round as if suddenly aware of the impropriety, silhouetted with her deelie-boppers in the dusk, more like a stag at bay than a hen returning from her own hen night. There's a long, awkward pause.

I find myself thinking that seduction is just being able to think of something to say at a moment like this. Something that isn't a terrifying indication of how badly you want to fuck. I can't think of anything.

I grip her firmly by the back of the neck and her mouth opens slowly under mine. She pulls my bottom lip gently between her teeth, then breaks off and walks abruptly up to the door.

'Night, night!' she laughs, way too loud, and I wonder if she might be drunk after all. I've followed her step for step and when she twists to say goodbye to me at the door I'm actually right behind her, kissing down hard on the back of her neck, her shoulder.

'Oh dear, oh dear,' she chides, turning in my arms to push her mouth into my chest at the open top button of my shirt. I'm holding her by her hip under her jacket and I push my fingers up inside her T-shirt to her bra, her nipple stiffening under my hand. She runs her hand down my chest till she reaches my belt, then, thank fuck, down to where my hard-on is straining through my trousers.

'I can't. My fiancé's inside . . .'

Oh, fuck.

'He'll be waiting up for me,' she declares in a stage whisper, looking off towards the road with a flicker of annoyance crossing her face.

Part of me knows that the moment has passed but then a wee voice in me thinks that if it had passed she'd be gone.

I kiss her hard on the lips and I can see the surprise in her eyes as I lift her up with a soft thump against the door, her head bumping gently against the little square of dimpled glass at the top, and I start pushing her skirt up. I keep expecting her to tell me to stop but it doesn't come, and I just keep pushing. She's running her tongue along my top lip as my fingers reach the top of her knickers, I tug at her tights, and everything just slides over her little bum surprisingly easily.

A light comes on in the house. Not the hall but back in there somewhere. I'm expecting 'We shouldn't be doing this . . .' at any moment, but I've got my cock out now and as I push up against her I suddenly have her full attention again. I've got my hand on my cock and I'm trying to guide it in, she's looking out to the road anxiously, which is odd when we can hear her fiancé moving about inside, but she's slippery to the touch, and just by pushing up from my legs I'm suddenly in her and she's biting into my shoulder as her deelie boppers start to rattle gently against the door.

I'm slipping it in and out of her, up through the bustle of her skirt, going as slowly as I can bear. The cold on the outstroke makes me aware of how wet my dick is getting between her legs. Suddenly the light goes on in her hall and I can hear someone shouting, indistinctly, like they're way back at the far end. Maybe her fiancé thinks she's just pissed and trying to find her keys, or . . . fuck it, who cares, I'm sick of worrying about other people. I can hear him in there, like he's moving towards the door, maybe just trying to work out what's going on. He says something, he's quite close now, but he sounds drunk and I can't make it out, and I'm fucking busy here, to be honest.

The shouting gets louder, he sounds drunk or something, an unhappy blah blah blah. She looks back anxiously and then wraps her legs round me really tight, suddenly moving up higher. I'm just holding her now and she's lost it, pumping her hips like a fucking jockey or something. I hear footsteps coming down the hall but it's too late because she's coming hard all over my dick, a gasp of warm breath steams up my glasses and her unmistakable loud moan breaks the silence of the night. This gets me right there and, as I start to shoot, I force open the letterbox awkwardly with my fingers and blast a load into their hallway.

There we are. That degeneracy should have seen everybody off. It's just you and me now; nobody else will have managed to get to the end of that bit. I don't think I've ever read it all the way through myself. Listen, while nobody's looking I'm going to try to explain all of human relations as quickly as possible. I imagine that you're quite young and idealistic – persevering with that porno and thinking that I'd a point to make. Well, if you could do something about what I'm about to say to you later in life, change the world, sort everything out, much appreciated. The question, obviously, is why I chose to include the sex scene. That, I think, is for the reader to work out, and then tell me.

We've a bit of a hangover from earlier times. People think of themselves as a 'self', a conscious being. In our modern market-driven society the 'self' is no longer the ego. It's our brand identity. Most of what we do is not to serve our ego, our own idea of ourselves, but actually to serve our status, other people's idea of ourselves.

We're the first completely market-oriented generation in history and it has destroyed our ability to be free and conscious. We're not the people we pretend to be. If I invented a time machine, I'd like to think that my first trip would be to go back and kill Hitler. In reality, I'd use the first trip to kill Piers Morgan's mother at the moment of his conception, and the second one to go back and check.

I remember even as a kid scouring those little brochures you'd get from Woolworths for my parents' Christmas presents. Like you, I moved on to express myself through the charities I supported, the bands I was into, even the people I hung around with. Around me grew a society where people would turn up for the half hour of adverts before a film and never complain, where we tried to express our individuality through the purchase of mass-produced goods. Even my favourite comedian, Bill Hicks, was peddling that 'individuality through smoking' thing. That was just an angle thought up by ad men decades earlier. People started to speak of the ads being better than the TV shows, somehow believing against all the evidence that the TV shows were the principal content and the adverts incidental. Now we understand that everything is to be marketed, even art.

I read the comic-book writer Alan Moore describe art as 'propaganda for a state of mind'. Who do we create propaganda for? Our equals? No, for the easily manipulated, for those we have contempt for. So to be an artist in the wholly marketed society is to have contempt for everyone. You prop-

agandise for your state of mind to others – and it's not even your state of mind. It's the off-the-peg set of opinions you got from the part of the culture you tried to buy into, from a set of people who were propagandising to you. They're not even your ideas. They weren't even theirs.

Of course, this doesn't make you happy, so you need to propagandise the chosen state of mind to yourself, through self-help literature, a term I use loosely here, to cover a whole bunch of stuff, including most religions and newspapers. What's the drive of your little internal propaganda office? Well, it's to sell the idea of you, to advance your status. By convincing people who you are too guarded to truly know about a bunch of ideas that you don't fully believe. And in any case, in a world of seven billion people what's your status, really? In truth, it doesn't matter any more than the charge on an electron.

Orwell imagined a coercive totalitarian state but Aldous Huxley probably made a better prediction of our current reality. In Brave New World *people are complicit in their own enslavement; they're into it. I think we can go further. It's not just that people are controlled by propaganda, or even that they enjoy being controlled. I think that people are now propaganda. People are no longer the things being controlled, they are the method of control, both of themselves and others. Of course, I've written this little serious passage here to advance my own status.*

I've tried to structure this book as simply as possible since it's supposed to have the energy and flow of a good stand-up show. Hopefully, everything is done here as I'd do it on stage

SCOTLAND'S JESUS

– a dip for you to regroup in the middle, a closing peroration, and even this little bit where I just kind of tail off mid-sentence as I realise that I already have your money . . .

SCOTLAND'S RUIN

1

ROYALS

One of the great tricks the British royals have managed to pull off is to have convinced everybody of their own irrelevance. They behave much like any big company, downplaying their influence, externalising their expenses, meeting with dictators, watching themselves sexually savaging hypnotised victims in the mirrored Aviators of their bodyguards, reporting back to superiors in other dimensions who appear to them suddenly in famous paintings, bad news causing their enraged overlord's face to seethe like a nest of startled snakes.

What's called pageantry and tradition – public events that only serve to highlight the relative charm of North Korea and the buying up of any golden sheds/tennis rackets that got missed by Michael Jackson – is just misdirection. It's the simple misdirection employed by a category of human being pitied by even the most denigrated monster of showbusiness, the stage magician. And that's all the royal family are.

1

Entertainers who've enjoyed the ultimate success by the most tried-and-tested route: aiming low.

Kate's pregnancy really brought the nation together. It was no longer just me thinking about her vagina 24/7. And call me old fashioned, but I thought it was nice to see a pregnancy announced – for most women in this country you only know they're with child because they've switched to menthol fags. Still, a lot of pressure for William. I suppose he's just hoping that he can be as good a father as his nanny was.

The birth was announced by putting a notice on headed notepaper on a wooden easel at the gates of Buckingham Palace – it's the royal equivalent of sticking a congratulations bed sheet on a roundabout. The law was changed because it was 'a historical anomaly that prevents the eldest child of the monarch from becoming the head of state simply because of their gender'. Unlike the historical anomaly that makes someone the head of state simply because they are born into a particular family.

Kate was a patient at the exclusive King Edward VII's Hospital. Aren't the royals wonderful? Even at their roughest they refuse to be a burden on the NHS. Kate had to endure eleven hours of labour. Which is more than the combined total the rest of the family has managed in the last twenty years. Being named George, her son will join six out of the past ten kings, exhibiting the imagination you'd expect from a family who have to be trained how to wave. Why think of a name at all? You won't get anything funkier than Prince.

Fifty armed police officers are to guard the new prince. Wow, in *The Omen* he only had that weird nanny with the

Rottweiler. There were few volunteers. Wouldn't it be cheaper just to employ decoys? He's a baby – that's pretty much the only time any lookalike has ever actually looked alike. The police will have to hand back their firearms once the baby boy becomes fully sentient, just in case a perceived slight leads him to lock their eyes with a haunting gaze, before causing them to vacantly push the barrel into their mouths and squeeze the trigger.

A Swedish magazine published eleven topless shots of the Duchess of Cambridge. It was the least erotic thing to have ever happened in Sweden. Why can't she just sunbathe topless on the balcony of Lord Linley's £15 million château in Provence like normal people? The British press will never publish pictures of Kate's tits. Due to the lack of space left after printing ones of her sister's arse.

The royal couple made a criminal complaint when the topless photos were published in a French magazine, and a French court prevented their further publication. The ban was soon extended to Italy and the rest of Europe, meaning the pictures were then only available to be seen on something called the internet. I sympathise with Kate feeling under constant surveillance. Thanks to my Catholic education I often can't shake off the idea my dead relatives are watching me. To be honest, I only ever feel comfortable masturbating while wearing a sombrero.

Maybe we should be glad that other countries take such an interest in our royal family – even if it's in this weirdly specialist porn way. Apparently, the Palace is so worried about Kate being papped that for the next few years she's to be permanently blurred during daylight hours by being shaken at high frequency by ladies-in-waiting.

The Palace was furious at the paparazzi hounding her like Diana, as royal protocol dictates that they wait till Prince Philip gives the nod. Surely the quickest way to stop the demand for these pictures is for the royals to finally go nude. I know what you're thinking. How about the etiquette of them breaking wind in public? Easy. Those dishwasher liqui-tabs with the dissolvable coating and detergent inside? Use them as suppositories and if it does happen it'll just come out as bubbles. At the moment protocol forces Her Majesty to hold farts in for years, only letting them out when the RAF do a fly-past over the Palace.

The supply of bland, feigned outrage about things like this seems endless. Eamonn Holmes on *This Morning* accidentally broadcast a photograph of Kate in a bikini. The programme had to apologise, as obviously the image should have been obscured by a list of suspected paedophiles. In fact, *This Morning* should really have had to apologise for showing an unblurred image of Eamonn Holmes. Eamonn's terrified the incident could prove yet another blow to his chance of a knighthood, a dream first dented in 2006 when the Queen accidentally pricked his casing with her sword and he whizzed about the room screeching like a punctured lilo.

In 2012 we had the disgraceful spectacle of the Diamond Jubilee. I've got to admit I was out on the streets cheering her on, although I'm not sure she fully appreciated my chant: 'Sixty years since your dad died, do dah, do dah!'

Michael Gove suggested celebrating the Jubilee by building a royal yacht. To be honest, I was just going to get her bath bombs or a book token but it was typical of Gove to try to show me up. I hate him, the unctuous, wet-lipped, Dickensian freak. If you asked a football stadium full of people if they'd like to see him kicked to death by a minotaur wearing plimsoles – so it would last longer – you wouldn't find a single person who wouldn't masturbate while it was happening.

I suppose a boat would be immune from a below-the-waterline al-Qaeda attack, as it's nearly impossible to get a watertight seal on your mask with a big, bushy beard. That's why the kids in Atlantis never get Christmas presents . . . but they don't cry about it. It's under the sea, so crying would be pointless.

A barge is totally in keeping with the royal tradition as typified by Liz and Phil. Engineering and shipping – you can't get much more German and Greek than those. And nothing says recession solidarity more than waving from a throne atop a golden barge. It looked like something Liberace would have rented if he'd taken a break on the Norfolk Broads. The whole thing was car-crash television, which made it strangely apt for a royal occasion.

Actually, I didn't go to see the flotilla as I failed to find a pair of clear-plastic water-skis to add a ghostly 'walk-on-water' quality to my Princess Diana outfit. Still, congratulations, Ma'am, on sixty years of feigning interest in an assortment of bland hats while a sycophantic media faithfully recount your occasional nondescript remarks as witticisms. Hers is an inspirational story. The meteoric rise of a girl born simply the daughter of a humble king. And let's not forget her role as Supreme Governor of the Church of England, a position that I've always thought must piss God off quite a bit. A little boy gave her some Werther's Originals to pass on to Philip. I understand that he prefers to receive jelly babies, as when the bag's destroyed by Special Branch in a controlled explosion there's less chance of the corgis getting shrapnel wounds.

All the royals were there – Princess Anne, the Duke of York, the Duke of Hazzard, Prince Harry, the artist formerly known as Prince, Lord and Lady Gaga, the Duchess of Cambridge, Duchy Originals Sausages, Viscount Biscuit and Sir, would you please put your trousers back on, the other diners are getting upset? We had a street party with jelly and ice cream and games for all the local children. It wasn't to celebrate the Queen's Jubilee – we were trying to flush out a paedophile.

Unemployed jobseekers were forced to sleep under London Bridge and work unpaid on the Jubilee river pageant. It wasn't all bad as they did get to watch the world's richest family sail by them in a golden barge. Sleeping under a bridge? That's Victorian, medieval even . . . what place could it possibly have at a royal event?

In honour of the Jubilee, Madame Tussauds unveiled their new waxwork of Her Majesty. Apparently, to re-create the effects of aging they just moved the old one next to the radiator for a couple of hours. I'm definitely going to take a look. Especially after the success of my trip to see the Prince Philip last Christmas, when I managed to land a couple of darts right in his chest. The Queen's waxwork has had its own special alarm ever since 2004, when the head was stolen and used to forge loads of big stamps.

God, the Queen must've been in a lot of photos – all the official ones, obviously, and she also loves to jump in the back of tourists' pictures for a laugh. We've all got our favourite memories of the Queen – mine was when she played Superintendent Jane Tennison in *Prime Suspect*. But she's great for tourism. Mainly because the sort of people dumb enough to want to see her are also the ones dumb enough to pay £5 for a warm Tango and a mechanically recovered meat hotdog, and £45 to watch roller-skating cats banging out the hits of Bucks Fizz.

By way of a gift for her Jubilee, the Queen was given 169,000 square miles of Antarctica, which she accepted with her trademark gracious scowl. Barack Obama said that while many presidents and prime ministers had come and gone, the Queen had endured. Barack, that's because you can vote for them, you prick.

Much is made of the Queen 'not being able to answer back'. As if a multi-millionaire with access to harems of devoted apemen and to drugs that let her taste chamber music really aches to be involved in a Twitter spat. The royals actually wield a lot of power. The Queen demanded to know why hate cleric Abu Hamza couldn't be deported. The police had been trying to arrest Abu Hamza for years but for some reason he just kept slipping out of the handcuffs.

I think it's great that the Queen's showing an interest in the sort of evil people who shouldn't be in this country instead of having them over for lunch, like she did with Robert Mugabe, Mswati III, Idi Amin, Hamad Al-Khalifa and President Assad. The journo who revealed the Queen's annoyance apologised for his breach of royal protocol, adding, 'From now on any pillow talk stays in the bedroom . . . Oh, no, you're not going to print that, are you?'

The royals have been unwell recently. The Duke of Kent had a mild stroke. He said he wanted to be back at work as soon as possible. It must have been more serious than we first thought, otherwise he would have remembered that he's never worked a day in his fucking life.

Meanwhile, Prince Philip was told he can no longer hunt as it may dislodge his heart, presumably knocking it into a place where it can receive its long-dead messages of love. There's a small metal tube that is holding his heart together. That would be a spectacular death, though, as he rips his own heart out to desperately load it into his shotgun.

I wonder if he got the NHS treatment we all get? I can't help thinking there's a twenty-year-old rugby player coming to in a field somewhere, his chest stitched like a 1950s football, barely able to get to his knees with his new nonagenarian heart.

I'm being unfair – the royals do pretend to do their bit for the community. Prince Andrew abseiled down the Shard for charity. He didn't raise as much money as everyone had hoped, as he made it down alive. He had to quit as Trade Envoy due to his links with a convicted paedophile, Jeffrey Epstein. A member of the royal family shouldn't be making us look stupid overseas. That's clearly the job of the SAS, the MOD and Jordan. The *Sun* referred to Epstein as the

'Paedophile Billionaire', which reminds me of the old children's rhyme: 'The grand old Duke of York, he had ten thousand friends. Not one of them what you might consider babysitting material.' Perhaps all paedophiles should be forced to have celebrity friends. It'd be an end to them being able to loiter anonymously around school gates. 'Get in the car, kids, quick! I don't like the look of that man playing conkers with Bono!'

Fergie took £15,000 pounds from Epstein. How many people would turn down fifteen grand, no strings attached, because it came from a child abuser? I mean, many people give more than that every year to clothing companies who tie six-year-olds to sewing machines. Fergie said, 'I would throw myself under a bus for Andrew.' He'd be very touched, if he knew what a bus was.

• • •

Prince Harry fought in Afghanistan. They kept that pretty quiet, didn't they? It's good that he went. If you want a flag waver for democracy it makes sense to send a prince. I say hats off to him. It's about time we had a few more positive role models for downtrodden ginger people. It might finally inspire them to turn their back on witchcraft.

Harry admitted that he's killed people, which should put an end to the question of whether he's really a member of the royal family. Saying that he's killed members of the Taliban hasn't made him a target; it's made all the gingers in the army who aren't surrounded by personal bodyguards twenty-four hours a day targets. It shows how sensible he's been, though. Nobody can get near you with a bomb belt if they have to be naked to get into your hotel room.

Prince Harry underwent hostage training in preparation for Afghanistan. It can't be easy having a royal hostage. You're supposed to cut off bits that serve no useful purpose and post them back. Where would you start? I hope he never gets killed on active duty. I hate to think of someone saying they need to inform his next of kin, then all the generals just looking awkwardly at the floor.

Harry was in the US to attend the Warrior Games. If he wanted to watch injured servicemen fight among themselves he should just nip down to any soup kitchen in the UK and throw a slice of bread on the ground. I've a fascination with watching disabled people play sports that has developed naturally from years attending Scottish Premier League football matches.

Cheryl Cole revealed she had a dream about marrying Harry. Something that in real life would surely end in a car crash bigger than her solo career. Cheryl doesn't seem like she'd fit in with the royals, but who knows, maybe the Queen also has a barbed-wire thigh tattoo. In most of my dreams I'm a princess as well – although I then unfurl into a half-horse, half-Gok Wan centaur who plays just behind the front two for Spurs, so I don't know what to think.

2
POLITICS

I suppose my political overview is that this five-thousand-year experiment to see what would happen if we let the cunts make all the decisions is going really badly. Anyone who doubts that power corrupts should have a think about what arseholes tall people are.

A key thing in the politics of Britain is the idea of consensus opinion. You see it in comedy where people say such and such a thing shouldn't be joked about but will joke about it themselves in private. They mean you can't say it in public because it would outrage consensus opinion. They'll maintain this even after you do it in a theatre to a few thousand people and nobody gives a shit. Even people in the theatre will laugh and think, 'You can't say that in public.' By which they mean the press will get a hold of it and jump on a stool shrieking and holding their little skirts. So *public opinion* really is almost synonymous with *media opinion*, and the dangers of that are pretty obvious.

For a comedian – someone whose job it is to deal with taboos and language – consensus is *the idea that you shouldn't talk about the world as you see it but instead about some socially agreed version*. But it shouldn't be a very hard decision. If you live in one of history's rare pockets of free speech it's kind of your duty to use it. Basically, the choice is between drawing freehand and colouring between the lines.

'Consensus' is something that most people have to make allowances for, yet, contrary to the word's literal meaning, most of us have very little say in what it is. The symbolic importance of public opinion is only allowed so long as people themselves are utterly marginalised. What's your real ability to influence the idea of what public opinion is on an issue? Tweet to two hundred followers, write a letter to the *Sun*, apply to be in the audience on *Question Time*? Who gets to decide what the public are saying they're outraged by or interested in? Well, Rupert Murdoch; corporate think tanks; the BBC. The public's idea of what the public thinks is almost entirely controlled by vested interests. Interests usually completely contrary to the public interest.

What is party politics in Britain? I mean, what *is* it? It's like support groups for a series of hysterical personality disorders that have embezzled other people's money to hold a competition to find the world's most boring sentence on board a crashing Zeppelin. Yes, anyone can vote. A fact that warms my heart each election day as I watch people yanking at the polling station door despite the obvious 'Push' sign.

People are outraged over plans to increase MPs' wages. Well, if they're not allowed to fiddle their expenses anymore then what are they supposed to do? Buy their own Kit Kats? MPs' current salaries are only £66,396 a year and when you take off how much of that goes towards housing, transport and general living costs, that only leaves them with £66,396 a year. We should remember that MPs do a very difficult job, and they do it very badly.

•   •   •

The Tories' role is essentially to make you eat their arseholes and simultaneously sneer at you for not knowing what kind of wine goes best with arsehole. As a Scot, whenever I hear George Osborne speak I instinctively start gathering up my belongings, expecting there'll be a knock on the door from the local sheriff telling me that this area is to become grazing land for sheep and that we're to be cleared off by dawn. And when I see Theresa May – wearing those weird clothes of hers – demanding the abolition of human rights I keep thinking I've stumbled upon a *Star Trek* I've never seen before (instead of the new version). I only keep watching in the hope that Kirk will come on from the side and punch her in the head. Meanwhile, in the audience Spock screams, 'MOTHER!'

Osborne's still insisting he never took cocaine as a student, claiming the only time he snorted at Oxford was when told stories of the troubles of the poor. Osborne on cocaine? Well, there's the answer to 'Whatever gave this tit the idea he could run the economy?' The man is so rich I can't imagine he'd use a rolled-up twenty. Maybe the deeds to Hertfordshire.

Cocaine makes you arrogant. If I were Osborne I wouldn't deny my cocaine past, I'd use it as a great excuse to cover for my array of God-given personality defects. I actually think it should be mandatory for the Chancellor to take cocaine, particularly before making the Budget speech. Instead of fiscal plans and growth forecasts he'd spend three hours pitching a screenplay he's writing about a dog who's been given his master's brain.

At the GQ awards Osborne joked that no teenagers reading GQ wanked over his picture. I think you're wrong there, George. I think the ones in Pakistan holding machine guns might do. If his current public image is the face that, after careful consideration, Osborne chooses to present to the world, then in reality he must be like a rogue android of Uday Hussain. He behaves as if Ted Bundy – experimenting with meditation – had found his mind conquered by a powerful telepathic crocodile. An amazing person, who, even when regularly advised not to sneer in public, just can't bring himself not to. The other plausible explanation is that his PR team is headed up by the time-travelling Sherriff of Nottingham. Perhaps the Chancellor's red box is actually made from Robin Hood's skin.

Osborne also announced that benefit payments are to be linked to the ability to speak English. So that's everyone on the dole in Glasgow fucked. Immigrants will lose benefits if they fail to improve their English at the same time as the government has been cutting language courses. It's got to the stage where immigrants are being taught English from the words spray-painted across their doors. Immigrants will only keep benefits if they take English lessons up to the standard of a nine-year-old. That's apparently the level necessary to understand barked instruction but with insufficient vocabulary to make it through a tribunal.

Foreign sex workers are being given free English lessons to help them understand the filthy things they're being asked to do. It's like a modern Eliza Doolittle: 'Why, I'll wager I could take a common streetwalker and turn her into a high-class prostitute!' It makes you proud to be British that we're willing to give immigrants a leg-up, as long as they're long legs attached to sexy bodies that offer inexpensive blowjobs.

The Tories also unveiled the new citizenship test and I'd like to see everyone take it. A question such as 'Which admiral has a monument in Trafalgar Square?' would give most *X Factor* contestants a stroke and enable us to deport the entire cast of *TOWIE*. At the top of each test would be the most pertinent question of all – 'Why the fuck would you want to come here?' They're also placing tougher restrictions on benefits to immigrants. We don't want our tax money spent on foreigners; we want it spent on going to the Middle East to pointlessly shoot foreigners.

Of course, what the Tories really think is 'Why don't we save time, stop all judicial decisions, the offering of evidence, defence arguments; just deport anyone who doesn't know that Starburst used to be called Opal Fruits.' The flaw in the idea that we need to educate immigrants about British history is that a lot of them have a better grasp of it than us, particularly of the bit where the British blew up their granny.

Immigrants often have to do totally different jobs from the ones they trained for in their own country. For instance, the bloke who took my appendix out told me he was a cleaner back in Poland. The guide to the test costs thirteen quid – save your money immigrants. If you want to be British then get pregnant when you're twelve and state that your greatest ambition is to see Rylan in a shopping centre.

The Tories are like some deranged sex killer who breaks down and tries to confess his crimes at a murder mystery weekend only to have people laugh and applaud at what they assume is his wonderful acting. At every Tory Conference the party outlines its priorities: building a Deathstar; killing Harry Potter; and creating a doorway into our dimension so the Many-Angled Ones can harvest our souls to the accompaniment of several previously unreleased Fleetwood Mac albums.

Boris Johnson usually gives a keynote speech that sounds like a Labrador having a ketamine-induced psychotic episode. And all the Tories speak of the Lib Dems like a celebrity speaks about the heavily sedated sibling they've sprung from hospital long enough to make up the numbers on *Family Fortunes*.

It's been said that Boris Johnson doesn't have the skills to become prime minister. He doesn't seem to have the skills to get dressed, but it happens. Sort of. Many Tories want Boris to lead them into the next election. I wouldn't trust Boris to lead me into a revolving door.

That said, Boris has done surprisingly well for a man who resembles a bouncy castle with Alzheimer's. On Mumsnet he described himself as a chocolate digestive: consistent and reliable. And also because rugby players regularly masturbated on him at Eton. If British politics were a film, Boris would be a character they'd put in just to sell toys. A teenager from Lancashire had Boris tattooed on his thigh. He might as well just have had two eyes tattooed on his arse.

It's amazing that these people can be so self-conscious without ever noticing how dreadful they are. Louise Mensch had a facelift. Hopefully, moving her mouth closer to her brain has helped but I feel terribly let down. I'd always thought she didn't move her mouth properly because she'd had a stroke. Who cares if she had a facelift? It's like people talking about whether Hitler dyed his moustache. She's an anti-abortion feminist, placing her on the list of great feminists somewhere between Peter Sutcliffe and Henry VIII.

The Tories have done a brilliant job while in power. The UK has suffered the worst fall in living standards since the Second World War. I'd add an 'apparently' to that as I'm not convinced downgrading from Sainsbury's to Asda quite compares with picking dead relatives out of the rubble. Cameron says it's time for Britain to show the world what it's made of. Though I'm not sure exactly what you can knock together out of debt and diabetes. He wants Britons to wrap themselves up in the flag – if you're living abroad I'd first quickly check it's not on fire. It was Oscar Wilde who once wrote that 'patriotism is the virtue of the vicious', but I suspect only as it was hard to find a publisher back then who'd print the word 'cunt'.

Still, at least the government's got its priorities right. Removing the 50p top-earner tax rate. It's just logic. Give the rich more money and they can ensure that troublesome youths are kept busy as gardeners, cooks and grouse-beaters.

FRANKIE BOYLE

The stories these automatonic politicians release to human-
ise themselves are always dispiriting. Cameron claims he's
completed every level of *Angry Birds*. Critics say Mrs Thatcher
didn't waste her time playing video games. A pity. Maybe
if Atari had pulled their finger out with their tennis-game
graphics the crab-nibbled eye sockets of hundreds of teenage
Argentine conscripts wouldn't now be staring mournfully
through the barnacle-encrusted portholes of the *General
Belgrano*.

David Cameron says he no longer cares about being popular. Well, that's handy. Cameron doesn't mind being unpopular
because steering through the agenda of big business is more
important to him than his political career and, like Blair,
business will reward him amply when he goes. Venezuelan
president Hugo Chavez died and thousands of Venezuelans
came out to mourn his death; if David Cameron died the biggest outpouring would be against the news over-running
when we wanted to watch *The One Show*. If Cameron died
tomorrow so few people would turn up you'd be able to cater
the funeral with a packet of Monster Munch.

• • •

I was shocked to hear of the death of Lady Thatcher. They say
the good die young, so I'd just assumed she was immortal. But
we must look at the positives. By all accounts, everyone now
has a little more leg room around that big oval table at SPEC-
TRE HQ. Sadly, many of her friends weren't able to attend
the funeral as they've been hanged at war crime tribunals.

SCOTLAND'S JESUS

She was cremated. That's what happens when you leave nobody in Britain who actually knows how to dig any more. The funeral brought central London to a standstill. The last time she managed that was the poll tax riots. I was all for a lavish, publically funded cremation. Right up until she died.

It's never a tragedy when a Tory dies. The tragedy is that they never truly lived. I'm not sure that Margaret Thatcher got many women into politics, in the same way that Myra Hindley didn't get a lot of women into hiking. All that Thatcher achieved was to ensure that people living in garbage camps a hundred years from now are going to think that Hitler was a woman.

A friend said of her that in retirement 'the nice side of her came out', something that only took eighty-five years and three strokes. It was speculated that Thatcher left an estate valued at £66 million in her will. It appears that she made her money by investing in a plastic-surgery company just before the Falklands War. She actually survived two attempts on her life. One being the Brighton bomb, the other when her assailant, after wrestling her onto an altar, stabbed the Daggers of Megiddo into her chest in the incorrect sequence.

Thatcher was desperate to end the days of governments bailing out lame-duck businesses, determined that they should stand on their own two feet. Hence the big switch from manufacturing to banking. Nick Clegg said, 'She drew lines we are navigating today', mainly as we weave our way home round the various companies digging up our gas pipes.

Several MPs mentioned Thatcher's beguiling sexuality. They say she had the ankles of a twenty-year-old – they were paperweights given as a gift by her chum General Pinochet. She did always come across as a very cold woman – I can't help feeling sorry for poor old Denis. Going down on her must have been like licking a lamp-post in winter.

Many of Thatcher's friends were quite emotional at the funeral. I think I saw a tear forming in the burning eye of Sauron, and when it was time for the cremation Simon Weston threw himself on, for old times' sake. The political guest list was a damning indictment of the inefficiency of the IRA. The only thing John Major ever did of note was having sex with Edwina Currie and not getting his head ripped off like a male praying mantis. I was surprised to see Sarah Ferguson there; I'd have thought she'd have sold her ticket on eBay. Fergie had a great time, though. She could finally sit in a room full of dictators without worrying if any of them worked for the *News of the World*.

Osborne cried. The world thinks George Osborne is a sensitive soul. Coincidentally, the man who sold him his new contact lenses has turned up dead in a forest. I think the stress of lying to us about having no money made him finally crack when the man in the silver cape stepped into the gold box. Osborne can apparently produce tears at will, just by picturing his policies' effects on the weakest in society . . . safe in the knowledge no one watching could differentiate between tears of sadness, and ones of joy. Of course, the saddest part of the funeral is when the curtain shuts around the body. I just have to be grateful that I found Amanda Thatcher's hotel window in the first place.

Seeing Cameron and Clegg united despite their warring parties reminds me of *Romeo and Juliet* – in that I hope this ends with them both killing themselves. The deputy prime minister now holds weekly radio phone-ins. So there you go – an answer to the question, 'Could any radio DJ be less popular right now than Dave Lee Travis?' It's not all bad though – as part of this job swap the Secretary of State for Business is now Tim Westwood. I can see this sneaking into other aspects of Clegg's life – when Cameron was reading a speech the other day Clegg punctuated it by shouting out 'Shabba'.

Clegg wants to create more construction opportunities to give young Brits jobs. I wonder how many media graduates it takes to make a docusoap about the qualified builders that will have to be brought in from Poland? He also wants to raise the speed limit to 80 mph – so that his motorcade can pass through any British city without being destroyed by angry locals.

The Lib Dems are now so extinct they'll exist only as a memory on *I Hate the Noughties*, being recalled animatedly but slightly inaccurately by Russell Kane in a segment even shorter than the one about me. Most people hate all three major parties. You'd do as well to put your X straight on to the polling booth and have the country run by a collection of portable balsa-wood cubicles.

A poll revealed the Lib Dems face becoming a political irrelevance right across the UK, not just in coalition meetings. As far as the coalition goes the Lib Dems now have leverage directly comparable to trying to open a five-litre tin of emulsion with a lolly stick.

It came as no surprise that MPs voted to keep the Lords – they were never going to get rid of a second house. Nick Clegg's worried without Lords reform he'll achieve nothing in this parliament. Of course you will Nick. At the very least you'll have destroyed your party.

As for Ed Miliband he has emerged as a leader more faceless than a highly buffed marble statue of a baby's arse, whose idea of passion is undoing the top button of his pyjamas. It's strange that he's so forgettable because he's got a face so weird it could make a police horse cry. I'd like to make different jokes about Miliband but we know so little about him it would literally be easier to put together a five-page Match.com profile for coastal fog.

At least no one can accuse Labour of a lack of policies or vision. I certainly felt the spirit of Nye Bevan sweep the party conference when Ed Balls rallied his troops with his proposal to part-fund a temporary reduction in stamp duty with money he hopes to raise by selling off the 4G phone network. 4G is going to be a boost for business. Salesmen tend to be way more focused in meetings if they have the technology needed to crack one off in a lay-by beforehand. Miliband has revealed he's afraid his young sons can access violent porn on his smartphone. To prevent this from happening do what I do – before giving the phone to the kids make sure you've deleted the contents of the history page.

I was surprised to learn Ed Miliband went to the same primary school as Boris Johnson. I'd naturally assumed both were failed prototypes for a Geppetto-like toymaker before he successfully made a real boy. Miliband's parents fled Nazi

Germany. But let's not forget Cameron's forebears were some of the first to describe Hitler as a monster – after he drank claret with the fish course when over for dinner.

Ed says he wants to make us 'One Nation'. Sadly that nation is Greece. We are united in one nation, one nation that thinks 'Not Ed . . . Anyone but Ed.' Sixty-three per cent of Labour supporters say he's not fit to be in Number 10. But he needn't worry; that never seems to have been particularly important.

Predictably, at the party conference the delegates stood for the leader's ovation with the weary disinterest and emotional disconnect of a nine-year-old Catholic boy unbuttoning his shorts for choir practice. Yet he shouldn't feel too smug. It's a fine line between a standing ovation and everyone just wanting to be first out of the room.

• • •

At a luxury five-star golfing resort in Northern Ireland the G8 leaders discussed plans to tackle world poverty, in much the way as you'd try to solve the AIDS crisis in a brothel. Syria was high on the G8 agenda. As far as arming the rebels goes, I think it's a good idea. As it must be some help militarily if our troops know exactly what's being used against them in eighteen months' time. We can arm the Syrian rebels just like we armed Afghanistan, with an agreement to pop back after twenty years to show them our new range of weaponry tastefully displayed in the roof of the local primary school.

The US claimed they would only arm moderate rebel groups, although it's possible these groups are only behaving moderately because they don't have weapons. How do you arm moderate rebels? With some strong coffee and the email address of the *Guardian* editor?

Frosty relations with Vladimir Putin and the Russians led to a slight alteration to the cutlery layout – at dinner it went fish knife, steak knife, Geiger counter. Putin wanted to show off his rippling physique in the lough next door. Surely time to deploy a rolled-up sock. I always do this when swimming – as you tend to get the pool to yourself if people think you've shat yourself. Cameron issued Putin with the ultimatum that unless he helps oust President Assad he will be forced to do nothing.

Cameron was called weak for not condemning Putin's re-election. In fairness, Cameron criticising dodgy election results would be like Richard Hammond calling someone a bead-wearing prick. Labour has criticised Cameron for being 'weak', and that means something coming from a party led by a man with the strength of a stick of month-old celery. Putin wept during his victory speech, a combination of raw emotion and tear gas wafting over from where the police were battering his delighted electorate.

Putin's had some work done around his eyes. I'm told he got all the laughter lines from repeatedly watching footage of the Chechen capital Grozny being indiscriminately bombed to rubble. I confess I've had the bags removed from under my eyes. Not for appearance; my pet mouse was just desperate for a leather armchair. This sort of thing does have its place. Friends of mine have a little boy and, without wishing to sound cruel, he had a massive nose. They got him plastic surgery and you barely even notice it now. You're too busy staring at his double-D tits.

Cameron travelled round India on his 'Sorry about that' tour. Dave went to promote trade, and to order a new chequebook after running out of patience listening to Beethoven while on hold for ninety minutes. At the start of his trip Cameron was struck by the visible poverty. And told the driver to take a more scenic route to Heathrow next time. Dave laid a wreath at the site of a massacre of three hundred protestors by British troops in 1919. And as a further mark of respect he waited a full hour before embarking on his sales pitch for the UK arms industry. Nick was left running the country. Though by now even he knows it's the equivalent of sticking a Fisher-Price steering wheel in the back seat in front of a toddler.

India is like an old couple that has won the lottery and Cameron just happened to 'pop by' with the head of HSBC to see if there's any gardening he can help them with or if they need anything from the shops. While in India, David wore a bandana, went barefoot and made a chapatti. So, that should make up for years of colonial rule and the Amritsar massacre.

Cameron's going to divert money from the foreign aid budget to defence, by cleverly rebranding missions as 'conflict prevention'. Fair enough. After all, the more people that die in military activity, the less there are left to need aid. But the charities aren't happy. There must be some kind of compromise. Surely it's not beyond us to invent a gun that fires rice.

Then Cameron and Prince Harry appeared together in the US. They were promoting the UK, although they missed the chance to use the slogan, 'Never a better time to visit . . . as right now we're not there.' They toured New York on a double-decker bus, allegedly the first time since last year's trip to Vegas Harry had heard someone shout, 'Room for one more on top!' Presumably, the idea of sending over a prince and a millionaire Etonian to try to persuade US businesses to invest in the UK was to make them think they can slash labour costs as we've still got feudalism. The Prime Minister announced Britain has clinched a deal with a US drugs giant to become a global test site for medicines. A global test site for medicines? That sounds pretty sinister. We could unwittingly become a nation of compliant drones, medicated to be distracted by shiny irrelevance while our rulers do as they please. When did they start?

3

TRANSPORT

I read an article in the *Guardian* recently about universities being corrupted by accepting money from fossil-fuel companies. I agree, but what about the *Guardian* accepting advertising money from those companies, or the ones that make cars or sell flights? Or what about the fact that it's printed on a tree?* Those things are so far off the agenda that you'd look crazy just for bringing them up. But that's because the press set their own agenda and their inherent contradictions obviously aren't on it. If I were to justify myself in the way the *Guardian* does – *I'll do adverts for all kinds of companies but make up for it by talking about how harmful their products are in my comedy show!* – I'd be considered at best a hypocrite, and perhaps even some kind of a lunatic. It's worth remembering that much as we say

* Hopefully, you're reading this on a Kindle or similar so it'll seem a lot less hypocritical of me.

we like to see orthodoxies challenged, we usually mean *other people's* orthodoxies.

I don't fly anywhere, or drive, and the whole fixed-grin, let's-pretend-it's-not-happening approach to global warming has given my adult life the sinister air of mid-period Hitchcock. It's a big reason I've never really felt I fit in with other comedians. It's hard to buy into anyone's carefully presented self-image when they take long-haul flights to international festivals every year. All these kooky shows about not being able to relate to your dad performed by people as indifferent to the fate of the Earth as a *Dr Who* villain.

It's bizarre in an age in which we are increasingly connected that we willingly choke our planet by taking unnecessary journeys. Flights and trains are packed with business arseholes going to meet people they could Skype, who spend the whole journey calling, texting, emailing home. The ultimate aspiration is to be 'jet set', jumping on planes to be away from our families, with headphones on to be away from ourselves.

How much bleaker do things need to get for these guys? Extreme weather events are becoming more powerful and more frequent. Most experts believe these are due to man-made global warming, although the prevailing opinion in the US is that it's God showing his anger at the lies spread by climate scientists. I'm sure we were all shocked by the Oklahoma tornado. Winds gusted up to 295 mph. To give that a bit of context it's the same wind speed that sees 90 per cent of Scots reluctantly leave a beach.

Britain is to face wet summers for the next ten years. I don't care as I've just invested heavily in umbrellas and sticks of rock that have baked in anti-depressants. When you cut through the stick of rock it says 'Buy an umbrella you miserable cunt.' It's going to be wetter than Michael Gove's bottom lip after a melon-eating contest. Actually, the government is forcing insurance companies to cover anyone at risk of flooding – which, if the Bible reports of Sodom are anything to go by, seems to be the entire cast of *Coronation Street*.

And Britain's winters could soon be colder because of increased Arctic melting. If the Arctic thaws it could reopen the Northwest Passage, till now just the title of a particularly bleak Preston-based erotic film. A bit of snow in Britain is great. As long as you don't want to go anywhere, come back from anywhere, leave the house or survive. The AA has warned people to take a special snow kit with them in their vehicles in winter – it comprises two bits of coal, a carrot and a scarf to make their car into a snowman.

I do my bit during the winter months, leaving out a cake I make from old bacon fat and seeds. Though a lot of the homeless are too proud to eat it. Hang it from your letterbox, then when they curl up for a post-meal nap they make a perfect draught excluder. Actually, I've been doing my bit for the homeless with my soup runs but to be honest I've never seen people so ungrateful for a bowl of gazpacho. If you're a pensioner worried about the cold weather, do the same as my neighbour and block out draughts by leaving your mail in the letterbox.

We seem to have problems with snow every year now – isn't it about time they started making paths out of salt? People moan when trains and flights are cancelled because of snow. It's like what they really want is pilots to come on the radio and say, 'Hi, it's probably too dangerous to take off, but fuck it, let's give it a go. Who's with me?'

Which reminds me, I'm supposed to be talking about transport. Rail fares are up by 11 per cent but I'm not going to slag the rail companies off. Some of these new services have great views from the top deck. How do these executives come up with that figure? My best guess is that they spend most of their days on their own trains, going nowhere, staring at the tracks heading off in to the distance. Subconsciously those track lines get processed as 11 per cent. So if we want cheaper train fares in future you know what to do: if you ever find yourself travelling next to a rail executive, pluck his eyes out with your plastic M&S spoon.

Rail bosses denied they've consistently missed performance targets, pointing out they've met the most important one, to get 100 per cent of price rises arriving on time.

Some people haven't been affected by the rise in rail fares. Justin Lee Collins, for example, won't have to travel to work ever again. I tried travelling free by hiding in the toilet. But it was too much faff squeezing behind that panel. And by the time we'd got anywhere I was hoarse from blowing people's hands dry.

Commuters have reacted furiously to the price rises. Many of them let their eyes glaze over as they pretend to read the *Metro*, lost in hypothesising the 'maximum damage for minimum bullet' route from their office to the roof, before emitting quiet sighs of relief as they picture being picked off by a marksman in a police helicopter.

But there's an easy way round it. Head to a collectors' fair and buy some Victorian tickets for the relevant line, then just by growing a huge moustache, popping on a top hat and dusting yourself in flour, pass yourself off as a ghost. Just be sure to remember to go, 'A Kit Kat, whooooooh, and a bag of Mini-ooooooooo-Cheddars . . . eddars . . . eddars . . .' when the trolley arrives.

The completion of the high-speed rail link between London and Birmingham could be delayed until after 2027. Meaning the announcement of delays is well ahead of schedule. We can be damn proud that we're able to announce delays to projects before they've even started. It's lucky it's a high-speed link or it would be delayed until 2079.

The high-speed rail initiative will reduce journey times to Birmingham at a cost of £32 billion. For that sort of cash I imagine they're going to achieve this by building a replica London somewhere around Wigan. I'm certain that any form of transport that can get you out of Birmingham at 225 mph will be welcomed by everyone. Passengers will now be able to say, 'How much? But it's just a coffee and a Snickers!' at previously unimaginable speeds.

Most of the track will be hidden, although I suspect a train going past at nearly 230 mph might just alert you as to where it is. There's going to be over twenty miles of tunnels – so at least there'll be somewhere for Cameron to hide when rebels decide to hunt him down like Gaddafi. The government would have more support spending £32 billion burying Birmingham under a tunnel and leaving the train on display. With the way the recession is going it'll end up just being a Megabus whose driver has a weight in his right shoe. The completion date for the new train route is 2033. They set that date because that's when the last remaining commuter starts working from home.

● ● ●

Hellishly enough, they're privatising the roads. Let's hope it goes as well as rail privatisation, so that in ten years' time we'll struggle to even get a seat in our own cars. More tollbooths will ensure traffic runs smoothly by having everyone standing completely still, waiting for a tourist to find £2.30 in change.

We already have roads only the wealthy can use. I mean, have you seen the price of petrol? Cameron called for us to show the ambition of the Victorians – so we should aspire to enslave half the world, masturbate at the memory of seeing a woman's elbow and die from mumps. The coalition wants to privatise the roads, NHS, schools, pretty much all services the state currently provides – soon the only way to get around will be to cut a hole in your pocket and leave a trail of 50p coins wherever you go.

I was stunned by rumours of price rigging by Shell and BP. It's totally shaken my belief in the benevolence of faceless multinational corporations. I just hope it's not true, as I can't stand the idea of being phoned twice a day by some prick asking me whether I've been mis-sold any premium unleaded. The government's right to have a go at oil companies for sneakily adding a few pence to petrol. That's their job. I decided to try living without petrol but it's hard. It took me over an hour just to push the car to the top of our street.

Cameron says the oil companies will face the full force of the law. If he takes as hard a line as he did with the bankers they could risk having their fuel-selling division separated from the one that sells pasties.

To be fair, oil companies have been very careful about price fixing over the last ten years; they only put up petrol prices when the price of oil rose and when it fell. Let's remember that forecourt petrol sales in the UK have actually fallen by 20 per cent over the past five years – a sign of the damaging impact that peace in Northern Ireland has had on the economy. It's estimated that the oil companies have ripped British motorists off by £300 billion. To put that into perspective, that's enough to fill the petrol tanks of almost a dozen cars. Despite BP being responsible for the Deepwater Horizon accident, the worst oil spill in US history, their profits have more than tripled this year. This seems reasonable; maybe there's just more of a market for dead pelicans than anyone knew.

Skint Britons are switching to mobility scooters to get round the high cost of motoring. Worries they'll block the pavements have led to immediate complaints from cycling groups. They may only be designed to go at 6 mph, but I got one up to 30 on the downhill. Only for a moment, though, then the caravan jack-knifed. OK, mobility scooters may not be that quick, but dey certainly get all dat sweet Day Centre pussy cumin to da TV Room winda, kna-wha-am-sayin, bro? If the price of petrol goes any higher, people might be forced to walk to the shops.

Lots of new road building has been announced. The most expensive road project will be the A14 between Huntingdon and Cambridge. Is this a priority? People are losing benefits but students at an elite university can soon visit a poisoned monkey and be back home in time to smash up a tea room. It will take three years for these roads to be re-built; think of all the things that could happen in three years – in three years that girl who ran off with her maths teacher will be on her seventh *Nuts* cover after having been voted out of *Celebrity Big Brother* for not being able to add up the shopping budget, but at least when she finally throws herself in front of traffic on the A1 it will be nice and smooth.

They always announce the cuts first, then the spending the next day – like a violent husband waking up the morning after and trying to make it up to you by buying you a road. No one has a job, so where are they going to on these roads? I suppose no matter how penniless people get they will still want to live as far away from their in-laws as possible. It appears that there are ten potholes for every mile of road in Britain. That's pretty dangerous – I'd recommend putting your Scotch into a beaker with a stopper before setting off.

More 20 mph speed limits are to be rolled out. Good, it's safer. Although journeys might take a little longer, we can just use the extended driving times as a chance to catch up on texts and emails. It'll mean more speed cameras but if you get flashed just do what I do. Rig up a magnetron from an old microwave to your car battery and fire it at the big yellow box to fog the film . . . even if it doesn't work, this lump now growing on my head means I look nothing like the photo they'll have of me at the DVLA.

You'll be fined if you use your mobile while driving, even if you're playing *Mario Kart* on your iPhone to practise your driving skills. Eighty drivers were sent police warnings after using mobiles to snap an accident on the M1 while driving. That's wrong. Far better to pull over, then change into your US cop costume, sneak up to the wreckage and stride purposefully from the flames like a T-1000. There's also to be a £90 fine for smoking at the wheel. They won't get me; I've just had my giant briar pipe electroplated as there's nothing in the rules about driving while playing the sax.

Recent research shows that one in eight drivers can't see properly in the dark. There's a simple solution – people with glasses should only be allowed to drive solar-powered cars. I sometimes drive when I've forgotten my glasses. It's not dangerous, as I'd know if I were about to hit someone by the panic in the sat nav's voice.

And speaking of dangerous driving, George Michael fell out of a car door on a busy motorway! Great to see him taking a break from singing to get back to what he does best. Poor George. He now has no choice but to do another world tour as it's the only way he can fund his next insurance premium. The police investigating the accident were looking for an explanation, then they saw George and went, 'Ah, right.' He's set to be the first person to be banned from travelling in the passenger seat of a car.

In much the same way as travellers favour a St Christopher, Middle Eastern truck bombers now clutch an effigy of George before driving at US embassies. I guess there was only so long George could look at the white line in the middle of the road whizzing past without wanting to hop out and attempt to snort it. There's been a suggestion that George tried to commit suicide. I don't believe it. After all, if he really wanted to hurt himself he'd have tried to park. It will be difficult to charge George with any kind of offence, as although he was caught on a speed camera going over the limit he has the unusual loophole defence that he wasn't in a car at the time.

George's car needed work after the incident, requiring a new honky-honky horn and a bit more custard in the radiator. He was rushed to hospital, regaining consciousness just long enough on his trolley to plough it into an A&E vending machine.

4

WAR ON TERROR

The *Batman* villain The Scarecrow produces a fear gas that gives his victims terrifying hallucinations. I was laughing with my kid the other day, saying that Batman got hit with the fear gas on an early mission and everything else is just the effects of the gas on him. The larger-than-life villains are just local teenagers being beaten to a pulp by this madman. He probably doesn't even put his costume on. The Joker is just some children's entertainer who gets regularly victimised during his flashbacks and The Penguin is a local pigeon.*

Really we've all had a blast of the fear gas. If you see a Muslim on a plane and think *terrorist*, that's a delusion. People walk about thinking they're going to be mugged or

* I don't really think this. Murderers (for good reasons) tend not to leave witnesses. The whole *Batman* story is just the revenge fantasy of a little boy dying in an alley.

raped, and do you know why? *They're pumping us full of fear gas, man, and it gets into the house through your TV.* That's why in the Western world, in these times of plenty and no real threats, we're governed by stress, the hormonal response to danger and famine.

Politics nowadays isn't so different from the way things were during the time of the Roman conquests. After their military victories the Romans held parades called 'Triumphs', in which the leader of a conquered territory would be paraded through the streets of Rome, symbolising in his person his defeated people. Compare this to Saddam and Gaddafi, and their very public deaths. Why did the Romans conquer? To provide popular support for their leaders and benefit financially from other countries' resources.

The Romans would enlist local leaders into their service by offering them money and patronage. It's not so different from David Cameron's relationship with our modern Romans. Oh, and the Romans aren't the Americans by the way; they're the corporations. The corporate interests that control the US thus control much of the world, like a modern empire. We're just one of those tribes whose leaders have struck a deal, so we ignore the plight of the imperial slaves who make our phones and we ignore our own people when they starve on our streets.

And, of course, we think of the Romans as this civilising force because we're a product of the Romans. They were barbaric brutes who crucified their enemies and got the popcorn out for prisoners being mauled by lions and bears. Similarly, we think of the corporate US as a democratising, civilising force because we grew up under its cultural occupation and have internalised its values.

There are the literal meanings of words and then there are the doctrinal meanings. The doctrinal meanings are what things are understood to mean *within the system* and are often different from literal meanings. So, for example, 'terrorism' literally means something done to terrorise the general population. Yet Britain and the US terrorise civilians every day with drone strikes and so forth, but we don't call this 'terrorism'. The doctrinal meaning of 'terrorism' is that it only includes acts against us, not by us – a pretty important shift of meaning.

I saw this recently when the comedian Stewart Lee wrote an article titled 'Where are all the right-wing stand-ups?' Lee's career since he got his own show is a bit like that episode where Father Ted gets an award and uses his speech to bitterly settle scores with everyone he's ever met. Anyway, it's interesting doctrinally, and interesting to me because Lee dismisses the idea that I'm a left-wing comedian. He wrote, 'The *Daily Mail* inexplicably demonises Jimmy Carr and Frankie Boyle as "politically correct left-wingers", yet to sensitive souls they appear callous, apolitical nihilists', but at the end of the same paragraph he concludes I'm 'too likely to be bluntly anti-war or pro-Palestinian to help Radio 4 out of its Trotskyite ghetto'. Of course, he's absolutely right in strictly doctrinal terms because doctrinally 'left-wing comedian' means 'a middle-class person concerned about social issues'. These will typically be people talking against the coalition, cuts and so on, but who generally draw the line at being bluntly anti-war or pro-Palestine.

Of course, to people outside a doctrinal system these things can look very strange. You'd have to explain to them that Stewart Lee – an Oxbridge graduate with a militant anti-piracy stance who appears on BBC Two punching up at the big targets of the day, such as the autobiography of Chris Moyles, mild-mannered comic Russell Howard and the ugliness of Adrian Chiles – is in fact a political comic. Someone like me, who was described by the *Daily Mirror* as a 'racist comedian' after a career of telling anti-racist, anti-war jokes, who took the newspaper to court and used the damages to help a Guantanamo Bay prisoner sue MI6 for defamation – I'm apolitical.

That's the real reason doctrinal thinking is encouraged: it fosters an ability to be deeply irrational. Possessing the moral agility required to say that blowing up civilians with flying bombs is not 'terrorism', or even simply to call Paddy McGuinness a 'comedian', is tremendously useful to a society like ours. Because we don't really need commentators to explain or reason; we need them to justify.

Of course, you're welcome to take Stewart Lee's view that the best place to criticise the behaviour of a crocodile is from inside its belly, perhaps in the hope that some day you will be so counter-cultural and innately radical that you'll be given your own show on BBC Two and the opportunity to edit Radio 4's *Today* programme. I'd argue that would never happen with a genuinely left-wing comedian who thought outside of the doctrinal system. Someone like Bill Hicks or George Carlin would have raised too many awkward questions. For a start, they'd have written an article titled 'Where are all the left-wing stand-ups?'

As soon as you enter into something doctrinally important, language becomes charged and contested. In Iraq, troops fighting the US were called 'insurgents' in the BBC coverage. That's quite an important choice of word, as an insurgency is something that happens against a legitimate government rather than, say, an occupying foreign army. In Libya, the troops trying to overthrow Gaddafi were referred to on the BBC as 'activists'. Like they were the sort of people who'd get a petition up about him, rather than publicly sodomise him to death. The doctrinal importance of attacks on American soil is semi-religious. Blood spilled in the Temple. The Boston bombers got the same publicity they'd have achieved by attacking the Kabul Marathon with a dinosaur.

The modern doctrinal era begins with the destruction of the World Trade Center. The Americans, in an understandable rage at the half-million dollar cost of the attack being funded by Saudi Arabia and carried out largely by Saudi Arabians, invaded Iraq and Afghanistan. It's good to remember that in years to come this whole period we're living through will be written off in a couple of sentences under the heading 'The Oil Wars'. 'Britain over-reached itself in the Oil Wars, was destroyed, and became Sexcamp 3 for Workers of Shanghai MegaProvince', the history books will read, as they sit in a petrol-soaked pyramid waiting to be lit as a warning signal to the Lastmen of the Garbagecities that their enemies the Crabmen have begun their final sideways march out of the sea.

Defence Secretary Philip Hammond said we should be proud of what we've done to promote peace in Afghanistan.

He plans to visit soon; he's just waiting till they've found a full Kevlar bodysuit in his size. We went into Afghanistan to get bin Laden and our mission there is more important than ever, now that we killed him, quite a while ago, in Pakistan.

The US is to open direct peace talks with the Taliban after more than a decade of war. Good to see the US has only waited twelve years and the loss thousands of lives before resorting to 'speaking' to them. The meeting will take place at the Taliban's new office in Doha – I like the fact they're opening new branches, so long as it doesn't get like Starbucks where you've got a Taliban on every high street. I wonder why they need an office – perhaps they're branching out and are going to start dealing with both insurgencies and van hire. I bet it'll be another call centre – we'll be plagued by the Taliban ringing up to ask if we need replacement windows or do we want to wait until after the car bombing?

There was outrage when burnt Korans were found at a NATO base in Afghanistan. They'd only been partially burnt. That's because the book on how to maintain a bonfire had been burnt the week before, on a bonfire of books about codes of conduct in sensitive areas. US soldiers don't understand why the word of the Koran should be precious, as most of the Christian beliefs they hold bear no relation to the literal word of the Bible.

It's thought Afghan soldiers were passing pencilled notes to each other inside the books they take with them to battle. US soldiers could never do that; it's hard to get pencil to show up on a cum-stained computer game. It's been said that because some people have burnt Bibles it's OK for troops to burn

Korans. I'll take that as giving me permission to restart my culling of Britain's bouncers. The books were burnt because stuff was written in the margins that the soldiers didn't understand. A translator is only $4 an hour, but they thought they'd take advantage of the spoils of war and splash out on a whole can of kerosene.

Can you believe it's over ten years since we brought freedom to the Iraqi people? The freedom to choose exactly who shoots and tortures them. Tony Blair says he's given up trying to tell people his decision to go to war was right. Instead he tells them it was 'complex and difficult'. In the way that lying is often more complex and difficult than telling the truth. An angry protester breached security at the Leveson Inquiry to call Tony Blair a 'war criminal'. Blair could easily stop people thinking of him as a war criminal. He just needs to have sex with a goat.

• • • •

So, Abu Qatada has finally gone. Mrs Qatada should move in with Mrs Hamza. As both their husbands are now inside that would basically give us an Islamic fundamentalist version of *Birds of a Feather* . . . Dorien comes round boasting that she's shagging the gardener and gets stoned to death. We'd all watch that.

Abu Qatada seemed to vary between being free and occasionally going back to jail, where either he would stay, be released or, ultimately, be deported. To truly get to grips with the twists and turns in that story what I did was every time

Theresa May began to speak I'd just gently hum the tune of the hokey cokey. I'd time it so she finished as I got to the 'in/out' bit, and then when I'd shake it all about I'd pretend I was being electrocuted by the Jordanian secret service. Jordan, of course, gave assurances that Abu Qatada would be treated like any other citizen and be entitled to a full trial by firing squad.

When your arch-enemy is a court of human rights it might be time to take a deep breath and think for a moment what that makes you. Abu Qatada was considered a threat because he spouts ridiculous, hate-filled tirades; if he were white he'd be presenting a phone-in on talkSPORT. To give you an idea how dangerous this man is it's believed he's radicalised almost as many Muslims as Tony Blair. As an extra security measure he was apparently given a dodgy compass so that none of his prayers would get answered.

Of course, we couldn't throw Abu Qatada out of the country just because he was 'very dangerous', otherwise there'd have been nobody left in the Cabinet. The Tories demanded that ministers ignore the courts and throw him out. I'm guessing the Tories might not be quite so keen on ignoring the courts when tens of thousands of disabled people refuse to pay their bedroom-tax fines. He was called bin Laden's right-hand man – and that was enough evidence to lock him up? If we called him the new Shirley Bassey could he get a plum variety slot on ITV?

A Welsh double-glazing salesman called Ahmed Abdulla has been stopped from flying to the US because his name is similar to the name of an al-Qaeda leader. The strange thing is that for the last ten years al-Qaeda leader Abdullah Ahmed

Abdullah has been travelling about under the name Dai Llewellyn. His attempts to organise atrocities keep being interrupted every five minutes by a housewife in Swansea who wants new windows fitted.

Islamic extremist Emdadur Choudhury was fined £50 for burning poppies at the last Armistice Day parade. I say, if he wants to live here he should protest about the occupation of Afghanistan the British way. Just shrug his shoulders and reach for the remote when it comes on the news. Burning poppies is a pretty piss-poor way of showing disrespect to our soldiers. It's not a patch on failing to give them proper body armour. Lots of people desecrate the two minutes silence. At least Choudhury had an opinion about war; surely it's more offensive when people just continue browsing through the Disney Store? How dare he publicly protest against the occupation of Afghanistan? Especially after all our efforts to bring it free speech. I'm told he'd planned a more lavish protest to bring the infidel British puppet government to its knees. But he couldn't buy the fireworks as his benefit cheque didn't arrive in time.

Abu Hamza was extradited to the US despite claiming he was too ill to face trial – well, to be fair, he does have one hand in the grave. My son was shocked. You see, I called his pet hamster Abu! Believe me, that's where the resemblance ends – his prosthetic, paper-clip paw's actually shaped into a trident . . . don't ask, but it's not cruel as all the animals involved get given badges to use as shields. I wondered why Hamza was so terrified of what the Americans will do to him; then I realised, he lived in Afghanistan for a bit. Actually, you'd think he'd have found a more realistic prosthetic in Afghanistan. We've been bombing them so long human hands must be left on garden walls like lost children's gloves.

Abu Hamza is a disabled man who commands great respect from his followers; if he conformed to our culture he'd be in a Channel 4 documentary about how no one wants to shag him.

He's been transferred to a US jail known as the 'Colorado Supermax'. Which is also the name of a feminine hygiene product for cowgirls. The European Court of Human Rights said it was satisfied Hamza would be well treated in America. Which in essence means that before flicking the switch on his electric chair the executioner will tell him to have a nice day.

Three guys in Birmingham were jailed for a suicide bomb plot. If I lived in Birmingham I'd be working on a suicide bomb plot. I'm not sure we should have been too worried about the destruction they could have reaped, given that they couldn't even manage to successfully burn the piece of paper with their plans on. With the plan of blowing up Birmingham they must be the only suicide bombers who've received financial backing from English Heritage. What could make someone who's raised in this country hate this country so much? Apart from being raised in this country.

This year we also had the Woolwich attack on Drummer Lee Rigby, and terror levels suddenly rose from 'not bothered' to 'holy fuck'. David Cameron returned from Paris immediately he heard that the black guy the police shot had actually done something to deserve it. Cameron activated COBRA, where the government show terrorists they're not scared by gathering behind steel doors in a bomb proof room.

An emergency meeting was held with Cameron, Boris, Pickles, Warsi and May – I wouldn't even trust this lot to make jelly and ice cream without starting a chemical fire.

The killer welcomed a Brownie guide leader, Ingrid Loyau-Kennett, when she approached him – he must've thought he'd completed his Death to the West badge. She wanted to keep him talking to prevent any further violence. That's unusual, as our scout leader always wanted to stop us talking. Usually with threats that nobody would believe us. Can you imagine being in her Brownie group now? Every time she asks what you want to do, you nervously gaze round to see if she's distracting you from a police marksman. Lee Rigby was wearing a sweater that showed a picture of a soldier being stretchered away with his thumbs up. There's a poster for the myth and reality of the job. You can tell his murderers were psychos; they left the body on a double red line. The killers' travel history is being analysed to find out how they got radicalised – I'm not sure whether that includes 'going to the newsagent'. People got off the bus near the attack to see what murderers looked like, as that bus hadn't run a night service for a while.

Nigel Farage said it was terrible this happened on the 'peaceful streets of South London'. Is he taking the piss? The police had to push their way past two stabbings and a shooting just to make the arrest.

It's interesting when people discuss whether a crime was motivated by religion or mental illness, as if those were two different things. Police found the training manual they used for the attack. George Michael's autobiography. The video of the jihadist ranting is going to be one of the toughest ever for Alex Zane to link to on the next series of *Rude Tube*. If it's an eye for an eye, who replaces the finger you blew off your own hand, you idiot? The killer said 'in our land' women see beheadings daily. In Lincolnshire? Are they still executing the left-handed? Still, thank God we held on to that Olympic feel-good factor.

The EDL, who named themselves after the way they text spell the word England, staged a drunken protest. I noticed the EDL rioters seemed to be covering their faces up. That's a bit Muslim of them. I think the EDL wanted to make a point about Muslims not respecting British law, and what better way to do that than to fight the police? Attacking a mosque in revenge for this murder makes as much sense as attacking JD Sports in revenge for Jimmy Savile. Muslim communities have to denounce these killings because they're so rare. If rich white guys had to denounce every death in their name they'd never get anything done.

We've got to the stage where 'asylum seeker' is an insult, whilst the government debates the vagaries of the term 'rape porn'. 'Asylum seeker' means you will be killed if you go home. And not in the 'I've had an extra pint after work' sense, though in some countries it will be because they had the pint, or went to work. 'Asylum seeker' is an insult and 'WAG' is a compliment. We have more sympathy for a woman whose husband might miss a header than for a woman whose husband might be missing his head.

• • •

More defence cuts have been announced. The Ministry of Defence insists operational capability will not be affected as the armed forces are already highly ineffective. If we're not careful we'll soon only have a military big enough to reflect our true status in today's world. We could slash Trident replacement costs by doing what Saddam did with his tanks and buying dummy stuff. I can't see any reason why inflatable submarines wouldn't work. BAE Systems is axing three thousand jobs. Oh dear, if only we hadn't toppled governments of its major clients. Sell the bomber jets to easyJet – at least it's a more honest way for our stag nights to enter Prague.

Cameron is insisting on the same number of new submarines to replace Trident, but Clegg wants fewer. I'd go with the Lib Dems. Look at our military requirements for the next fifty years – it just has to be easier hauling two subs across a desert rather than four.

And on top of cuts, stolen military kit worth millions is being sold on eBay. I've bought night-vision goggles, part of my plan to gain the psychological advantage on *Mastermind* by choosing 'The various sleeping positions of John Humphries' as my specialist subject. Meanwhile, ex-military chiefs have been caught offering ministerial access for money. Arms traders shouldn't lobby. They should follow the proper channels and just show off their coolest stuff in conflicts, because for defence ministers CNN is basically a shopping channel. Indeed, many US arms dealers' catalogues are made up almost entirely of photos from Afghan wedding photographers.

A CNN journalist said she'd like to urinate on a dead Afghan. Luckily, she works with Piers Morgan so she can get a mocked-up picture of her doing it. I'm willing to offer my services if she'll accept a put-on accent and a bucket of spray tan. I'd happily kill three thousand of her friends if it helps? This is not the first time I've seen a video of four American lads pissing on someone, although I must say the dead Afghans exhibited a more realistic enjoyment of it than the girls on Xhamster. These Afghan soldiers were told they would meet a group of virgins after they died, and it looks like that was correct. We're a strange society that pixilates the willies in that footage but not the corpses. Why would soldiers at the end of a tour of duty wee on dead bodies? The probable answer is that they'd simply run out of cum.

I liked it when al-Qaeda posted pictures of an all-female unit of terrorists training on an array of weapons. They've been dubbed the 'Burkha Brigade'. I doubt they'd be that effective in the UK, because if a team of them were spotted crouching down behind a wall the neighbours would be straight on to the council reporting that someone has been putting their black bin bags out on the wrong day.

A lot of our general culture is war propaganda. Did you see *G.I. Joe*? It's a film based on a children's toy. I've got a few ideas in the same genre that I'd like to pitch. How about *Kerplunk*? Bruce Willis's children are suspended between two skyscrapers by enormous lengths of steel piping, creating a net that they rest on. Willis has to remove one pipe every hour or his children WILL die. Or what about *Hangman*? We could splice together archive footage of the death of Saddam Hussein with some random clips from *Countdown*.

We're told that terrorists are talking to each other through online games like *Call of Duty* and *Halo*. Al-Qaeda should be careful; these shoot-'em-up games can desensitize a person to violence. Sad we've only found out this link between games and terrorism so late in the day. I can't help but wonder whether the world would be a happier place if only someone had had the sense, in the 90s, to ban Jenga.

• • • •

North Korea announced nuclear missile tests targeting America but they're purely for scientific reasons – they want to find out what happens if they blow up America. The US government has warned North Korea to stop making threats, or else they're going to fucking kill them. Some North Korean generals suspect their delivery system is too basic to get a missile to Washington, believing the US will probably recognise the stamps.

The West despises North Korea as a dictatorship. Dictatorship is when someone tells the people what to do. Democracy is when the people get to choose who tells them what to do. Naturally, we all laughed at the scenes of national mourning in North Korea when Kim Jong-il died, until Thatcher went and we did exactly the same. We didn't even have the excuse that we're delirious from hunger. Oh no, actually we did. It's a communist tradition to have endless TV footage of the embalmed corpse of a tyrant at rest. We don't do that here – we'd rather go for endless TV footage of his begging for mercy before being shot in the face.

Kim Jong-un has a girlfriend. By all accounts, Kim has spent weeks getting to know her, having had her family surgically implanted with bugging devices. I haven't seen her dating profile but I'm guessing it includes: 'Hobbies, venerating the great leader, collecting pebbles, trying to stop my imagination morphing people I meet into giant talking items of food.'

If there were a nuclear conflict in the region North Korea would be left a barren wasteland. So they've nothing to lose. David Cameron is very concerned that they can reach us with their missiles – to be honest, Dave, I think you should be more worried that there are plenty of people in this country who'll be able to reach you with a stick. Let's face it – if North Korea blow up the government before we do then we should all be ashamed of ourselves. I'm not that worried about Korean missiles hitting us here – mainly because I used to have a Korean car and it could barely reach Sainsbury's.

Our government assures us Britain is ready for nuclear war. Really? We weren't ready for snow in April. With the way things are going you could well be reading this on a scrap of scorched paper you're using to bandage your weeping radiation sores as you fend off the other mutants with a spatula. Nuclear war in Scotland wouldn't change much, as we already spend most of our time indoors with the curtains closed, the windows shut, avoiding all contact with other humans and never eating fresh fruit or vegetables, or drinking water. It seems the only difference is that we'd be pissing into Coke bottles at the request of the government rather than because we can't be arsed getting up off the couch. Cameron was also scaremongering about Iran having missiles that could target

Britain. Actually, they barely have anything that could reach Israel. If they do target us we have two choices – either diplomatic talks or sending scientists to help them build a missile capable of going far enough to hit America.

David Cameron's released this information so we can act ourselves – so lock your doors at night, leave a light on so Iran thinks you're in when you're not and report any strange missiles you see in your area.

Barack Obama said the US government requested that Tehran return the surveillance drone captured by Iran's military. I hope he's not holding his breath as the Japanese still haven't returned that bomb from Hiroshima. What's wrong with Iran? Why are they so paranoid? Anyone would think the West had at some point overthrown their democratic government and installed a brutal puppet, or cynically perpetuated their war with Iraq by selling arms to both sides. Israel is doing all it can to stop itself being a target. Well, everything short of not bulldozing Palestinian homes and building on land they promised not to.

Israel has apparently been assassinating Iranian scientists. Let's hope they don't try to assassinate any of ours; they'd have to queue behind anyone who ever bought a D:Ream album. Iranian clerics are denying Tehran wants the bomb, claiming they only need lumps of weapons-grade uranium for throwing at particularly promiscuous women.

Israel will have 'no greater friend' than the US in pursuit of peace in the Middle East, Barack Obama promised. Of course, Israel need a multi-billion missile defence system from America – how else are they going to protect themselves from children throwing stones? Israel are worried about Iran attacking them but it's all academic anyway – America will still beat them both to the Most Murderous Regime in the Middle East Award again. The US is determined to bring peace to the Middle East and they don't care how many millions of unarmed shepherds, women and children they have to brutally kill in order to do it.

Israel insists it's targeting specific militants. Though in bombing the most densely populated place on earth that's a bit like finding a bee hive but only targeting specific bees by using a mallet. It's easy to badmouth Israel but the fact is that one way of reducing the risk of injuring civilians is to reduce the number of civilians actually around to get injured.

Netanyahu insists there could be a Palestinian state. But not till Israeli settlers have nibbled so many bits off the West Bank that the Palestinians can only fit into what's left by stacking themselves up like a motorcycle display team.

There's understandable concern in the UK that the conflict could spread across the Middle East. It would clearly be a calamity – another 5p on petrol. Basically, the Palestinians took a wrong turn back in 2006. They were offered a free democratic vote, and they went and voted for the wrong party. Let's look at this historically and realistically. Germany should buy Crete from Greece and give it to one or other of them.

Like most of the international community I'd like to see a two-state solution, where people live side by side. I'd like to see one state occupied by Israel. An aggressive, destructive military power who stops at nothing to bulldoze and bomb their neighbours. And I'd like the second state to be Essex.

But congratulations are due to US Secretary of State John Kerry on getting the Israelis and Palestinians in the same room together. Apparently his trick was to give the Palestinian representatives a room first, then put the Israelis in one next door, and wait. Initial talks went better than expected due to Kerry's radical approach. He told Middle East peace envoy Tony Blair they were being held in Turkey. Blair's not had the best record in his role. He has more the air of a man sent ahead to check stabling facilities for the Four Horsemen.

Allegations of chemical weapons being used by the Syrian government have raised the possibility of Western intervention. To summarise, the Syrians are killing each other with the wrong type of weapons, so we're going to kill them. Syria's war is much easier to bear if you think of the past two years of death and destruction as an elaborate opening ceremony to World War Three. Poor Syria. Now the papers have started printing pictures of dead children, maybe we will see the ones killed in US drone attacks, or shall we wait for the hardback coffee table book? The heartbreaking photos have opened the world's eyes – if you want people to care about your dead children make sure they die in a way that's not icky to photograph.

One of Syria's tactics is trying to destabilise Iraq by flooding it with refugees. A bit like a humanitarian version of Buckaroo. Interesting how it's often the militant Islamists whom Arab dictators are killing; wonder where they got that idea from? Looks like any invading American force would have to start their mission by saying, 'Now . . . this is awkward . . .'

I can't believe our MPs voted not to back the US. The UK's going to look as stupid as back in the 1960s, when we chose not to follow them into Vietnam. As I write, we're being told that, unlike Danny Dyer, America must now act to maintain its credibility. The UK said any bombing would only be for 12 hours – but remember to always round projected war timings up to the nearest decade. The big question is all about UN approval. Does the West need to bother pretending to get it or not? It's all about making surgical strikes. From 100 miles offshore. Like having your appendix removed by a circus knife-thrower.

Things are now so bad there that Bernie Ecclestone's put in a call to President Assad about hosting a Grand Prix and we've been dropping in troops as 'advisors'. It's all perfectly legal so long as when they shoot someone they say 'I advise you to die.' In some ways I suppose Syria's lucky. Imagine how bad things would be there without the years of skilful work by Mr Blair.

Blair says we must take a stand against al-Qaeda in North Africa. Although obviously he doesn't mean that he personally will be taking a stand as he doesn't want to get shot. He'd like you or your kids to get shot, for something that the untrained eye might think should possibly be the business of, and I admit I'm going way out on a limb here, North Africans. Cameron's warned that the UK could be fighting al-Qaeda there for decades. Or to put it another way, until the oil runs out.

Cameron even did a tour of North Africa's most dangerous spots. That's a bit like the head of an abusive, violent family visiting the foster homes all his grandchildren have been placed in, then lecturing them that they need to behave if they're ever going to get anywhere. Cameron visited Martyrs' Square in Tripoli, where the riots began. Wonder when he last popped in on Tottenham?

No one seems to be concerned that we're just about to launch a war against Africa. I'm guessing the public will only begin to take notice when a cluster bomb intended for a primary school hiding enemy combatants accidentally kills a baby elephant. If the war in Africa escalates, Broadway musicals will be uniquely placed to react to events with a topical show by simply performing *The Lion King* and *Miss Saigon* in the same theatre. This might be the only campaign where the RAF drops red noses before doing a loop and then launching missiles.

Western leaders have expressed their support for the new government of Libya, telling them it's a time for calm, reflection and rearmament. Hopefully, the rival clans will now be brought together by their rich shared history, going back almost sixty years when their country was created by the French and the English whipping out a pen and ruler after a piss-up.

Libya is far from poor. Apart from its oil, being 90 per cent desert has made it the world's largest exporter of egg timers. They could now make a fortune from tourism. The beautiful coastline and Roman ruins make it ideal. Plus all the random weaponry would be ideal for men on stag weekends to rent for drunken camel shoots.

The campaign was a triumph for NATO, their in-house magazine praising the campaign of air strikes with the headline, '4 schools, 2 hospitals . . . but no weddings this time!' The campaign does send a strong message to the remaining tyrants in the Middle East. Look what might happen if you drive too hard a bargain with our oil companies.

5

EUROPE

It's difficult to understand why Britain and other European countries can't agree on anything. It's as if they each speak a different language. Why is Europe such a big issue? The entire world is pretty much run by a network of banks so the whole question of Europe is largely about whether or not we want access to a slightly wider range of cheeses. One reason for its importance politically is that it's a kind of last refuge of racism. Not a lot of those anti-Europeans want us to leave Europe so we can join Africa.

The other reason is that the City of London is essentially a big tax haven. We launder a lot of the world's stolen loot here in Britain, and our politicians view Europe as regulation. The general attitude is that of a pirate ship being asked to sign up to regular health and safety inspections.

I'm in the happy position of hating both anti-Europeans and most of Europe. I remember that whole guilt trip at the time of the Greek bailout about how the Greeks had no work ethic, the Spanish didn't work long enough hours, and they were all being bailed out by hard-working Germans. Have you been to Germany? It's a fucking nightmare. Everybody works the whole time so they're all stressed out and the smaller towns have almost nothing in them as nobody has any free time in which to do anything. The Greeks are being punished for attempting to lead some kind of life worth living while international finance tries to persuade them of the fun they could have as a work camp.

Cameron says the in/out referendum in 2017 will settle the 'European question' although it's still to be decided whether there will be a third option of shaking it all about. But it all depends on the Tories being re-elected. So the chances of the referendum happening are about the same as Ireland building a space station. Besides, 2017 is years away. We don't know what the world will be like then. Other than that we'll be part of China and everyone from Morph to Optimus Prime will be a convicted nonce. Forty-three per cent of people would answer yes to 'Do you think UK should remain a member of the EU?' I suspect they could get nearer to 95 per cent just by subtly tweaking the question to 'Have I not got any idea what this is really about?'

The problem is there's no 'control' UK, in other words there's not another country that wasn't a member of the EU to compare things against – in the same way I don't know how my life would have turned out if I'd not had a kid, as there's no control Frankie. Sadly he died in 2006, on the rim of an erupting volcano in a knife fight with his nemesis, 'control' Phillip Schofield.

When people have no real choice you start to embrace the irrational. That's why the very poor are often preyed on by mediums and spiritualists. And that's exactly what voting for UKIP is, really: the sort of irrational decision we make when we're powerless. UKIP are political tea-leaf readers encroaching on the territory of politicians engaged in a sophisticated long con operation, in the same way clairvoyants used to infringe on the swindle being worked by the Church.

But what a great year it's been for Nigel Farage. After all that Olympic nonsense, it's about time the St George's Cross was reclaimed by arseholes. UKIP fielded so many candidates in local elections they had to admit they didn't vet them. They got them like pub football clubs get a team on a Sunday morning – 'Hello, have you got your own shorts? Right, you're the candidate for Haverford West.'

A UKIP candidate was shown with a knife between his teeth and holding a Union flag. For one glorious minute I thought he'd killed Geri Halliwell. UKIP's politics are a little vague but I think the main one is to take the trillions wasted on diversity officers and use the money to fund a time portal taking us back to 1972.

UKIP have pledged to get us out of Europe – which might be a bit tricky given where the country is. David Cameron's been warned he has to take Nigel Farage seriously, a hard task given that he's got a face like an indignant gecko. The likes of UKIP have some nostalgic view of a lost Britain of supportive communities. Sorry, bampots, but these communities still exist; it's just that they're Muslim and Sikh. Amusingly, Farage tried to escape from a gang of Scottish protestors by hiding in a pub. Which is like trying to hide from a lion by putting on a zebra costume.

Cameron called UKIP supporters 'odd'. Which is a pretty fair description of anybody who thinks the Tories are too pro-Europe. UKIP candidate Geoffrey Clark's manifesto says foetuses with Down's syndrome should be aborted. There *is* an argument for the compulsory abortion of some foetuses but how on earth can you tell in the womb if a baby is going to grow up to be a UKIP candidate? As Geoffrey's already in his late sixties, I'm sure he'll allow himself a chuckle at the irony when his family smother him with a pillow so he's no longer a burden on them.

After weeks of riots, Greece was burning. Troubling times, but it must have smelt gorgeous. Our rioters were criticised for stealing things rather than making political points; the Greeks burnt down Starbucks. I actually have more respect for our rioters coming away with more than pride and a travel mug. It's sad to see the inventors of democracy doing so badly at it – it's much like watching the English play football.

In their election, Greece had no clear winning party and was reluctant to form a coalition. It's quite something when a country of homeless people setting fire to bins don't want to make the same mistakes as the UK. The Greek parties say a coalition would be a tragedy. This is a country that defines tragedy as pulling out your eyes in exile after killing your father – the difference being that with our coalition you'd be expected to work through your blindness and set up a co-operative to bury your father.

I've always said that their outgoing prime minister Papademos wasn't good with finances. Ever since 1993, when band-mate Pliers made off with all the royalties from their hit 'Tease Me'. I'll admit I'd no idea the Golden Dawn were a Greek neo-Nazi party. Especially as for the last five years that's where I've been getting my lemon chicken and spring rolls from.

The £110 billion bailout to save Greece was called a failure hours after it was signed off. A sad day. Greece used to be a proud and progressive country, just 2,400 short years ago. The IMF are worried about economic growth – to be fair, it's quite hard to go shopping when a balaclava-clad teenager has just thrown a petrol bomb through the menswear department.

Greece invented maths, democracy, homosexuality and philosophy. Then nothing for a long time. Now they just break plates. They're like a genius who's had a mental breakdown. I think a big problem is that one of their main industries is smoking under trees, while a feral cat scratches their chair leg. Everything there is now up for privatisation. I want to buy Lesbos because I've got an idea for a theme park. Of course, not everybody's suffering in Greece; at least there are now a couple of teargas billionaires.

British tourists have slept with so many Greeks the whole country is now officially considered an 'ex'. We've got a bunch of their stuff, they owe us money. And there's more of our spunk in their sewers than in every sperm bank in the UK.

Angela Merkel was greeted by thousands of angry protesters when she arrived in Greece. There was an awkward moment when protesters picked up bricks and petrol bombs

– then started running around trying to find something that hadn't yet been vandalised. Fortunately, the majority of Athens's most valuable treasures weren't affected – as the riots didn't come very close to the British Museum. The only comfort in seeing the greatest civilisation the world has ever known crumble into decay is the knowledge that one day the same fate will befall America.

It's quite sad, really – we're threatening Greece to accept our help when they yearn to be strong and independent, as if we're forcing a £50 note into the bloodied, trembling hand of a sobbing teenage prostitute. It's a shame that China will finally take over Europe by buying it as I was rather looking forward to seeing the attack formations of their swarms of robotic bees. Greece, if you think you're angry now, just wait until you're eating egg foo young out of a pitta bread.

Actually, I'll be interested to see what happens – round my way every place that goes bankrupt gets turned into a pound shop. Greece could end up being 50,000 square miles of scourer sponges and Pritt Sticks.

In Cyprus people were unable to withdraw money, mainly because there were fifteen camera crews standing in front of every bank. A Cypriot MP said Cyprus was being raped by Europe; then once Ryanair flew all the stag parties back to Birmingham she discussed her financial problems. Rape's not the correct analogy; there's no one inside Cyprus because Cyprus is frightened they will be killed if they say no, but I'm sure we could arrange for an American occupation if anyone can find some oil.

There are great fears that Cyprus will end up under the control of the mafia, but Europe's intervention isn't yet guaranteed. In debt to the Russian mafia or in debt to Europe? Tough choice. Face threats of a slow death by radiation or be made to watch Angela Merkel make small talk over a vol-au-vent whilst she forces your daughter into prostitution.

6

SPORT

Sport exists because we're so emotionally damaged and distant that we need a shared narrative to be able to relate to each other. You'll have done that thing where you find yourself round someone's house and the telly is on and you don't know each other that well, but you interact by making shared reference to this third thing? Sport is just a larger societal version of that, playing pointlessly in the corner of the national imagination. A neutral conversation piece, a very basic way of making sure you're not talking about politics or love.

There's that old Nick Hornby idea of footballers being our chosen representatives on the pitch. I wonder if sport might not actually be about celebrating the worst in ourselves. Just as *Star Trek* can be seen as being about our suspicion that we would achieve more if we let our impulsive, psychopathic side (Kirk) dominate our rationality (Spock), so sport might be a fantasy about a life unburdened by intellect giving us the opportunity to bawl our approval for someone who – in a world of ever-increasing knowledge – has focused on running and jumping. We've all looked into the unknowing eyes of a dog and envied him for not being worried about anything past dinner, sex and exercise. It wouldn't be so very different if you looked into the eyes of Jamie Carragher.

The cultural weight that sports are given is deeply irrational. The BBC drew up plans to deal with news stories during the Oympics – only major stories would interrupt the Games. That could have led to some interesting sports commentary if there'd been a tragic event not deemed major: 'There goes the starter's gun, which reminds me, if you have a child attending school in the north-east you might want to turn to BBC Two now.'

The marketing of sport with its cod nobility is just silly, really, and it's remarkable how the reputation of things such as the Olympics survive the evidence. It's been revealed that much of the 2012 Olympic merchandise was made by children in China. For them the five Olympic rings mean the ones around their ankles, wrists and neck that stop them straying from their workstations. Finally, Wenlock and Mandeville make sense – they were created in the nightmares of tortured Chinese slave children. They're the physical manifestation of despair. You've got to respect the Chinese; they can get their kids to make soft toys with enough consistency to start a commercial venture. I can't even get my kid to put on his shoes when I want to leave the house.

A florist even had to take down five tissue-paper rings as they breached Olympic trademark laws. Excessive? I'd rather not say as I'm currently being threatened with action for putting down my coffee mug a few times without a coaster.

There surely needs to be a handicap system to stop the same teams always topping the tables. I'd suggest competitors have to do events wearing their country's previous Olympics medal haul. Then Team GB could be spurred across the line by what look like half a dozen glistening golden armadillos or, depending on the event, shimmering dead swimmers. Also, I don't see why the last day of the Olympics shouldn't be all the gold medallists playing dodgeball till we have an ultimate champion.

Seventy-six per cent of people say the Paralympics lifted the nation's mood. It made me more depressed. I can't throw a discus and I've got arms. David Cameron said the Olympics and Paralympics have had as much impact upon the national psyche as England's World Cup victory in 1966. I think they've had even more impact, as Team GB and ParalympicsGB won without cheating. The big question is how on earth is Rio going to follow London 2012? My guess is by building some stadiums and holding some sporting events inside them.

Olympic Chairman Lord Moynihan says more state-school kids need to get into competitive sports. He's right. We were always encouraged to do cross-country running in our school. Especially when we found out that the priest's sandals had such poor off-road traction. So many memories: 'You've left your bag at home? Well, you'll have to do the lesson in your vest and pants then.' It didn't matter whether it was maths, English or history. My school was very sporty. One class friend even managed the 100 metres in under eight seconds. I always wonder if he'd been taught more academic stuff whether he might have got a job and not leapt off the top of the BT Tower.

The Olympics created a new batch of sporting celebrities. Jessica Ennis was given the keys to Sheffield, although she'll have to wait until they find them. They haven't bothered locking it for years in the hope that someone might steal it. I'm also a big fan of Mo Farah and the Mobot. As you can do it, then dip your torso in a bin-full of soapy water, before running down the street at the head of a trail of giant bubbles.

And what about *Splash!*, Tom Daley's ITV show? It's hardly the most exciting format they could have got from the Olympics, is it? I'm sure there'd be way more viewers for a celebrity version of Munich 1972. You probably expect me to be down on *Splash!* but I reckon most ITV shows would be improved if contestants had to jump off a ten-metre board. Though they have messed up a perfectly good format by including a pool. Tom Daley – bless him! – every time I see him near the edge of the pool I just want to put armbands on him.

Tom Daley's an ideal trainer as he feels no fear, being just a composite of molecules assembled by the telepathic will of the nation's lonely aging homosexuals. Tom doesn't let anyone sponsor him. Part of his plan is to use his deals to help nurture athletes in poorer countries. That's why he went with Nestlé, as their aggressive promotion of powdered baby milk helps ensure only the hardiest of sub-Saharan tots survive. Still, maybe Tom needs to make as much money as he can while he's got the chance, or in years to come he'll be on street corners offering to hurl himself into a paddling pool for loose change.

The title brought to mind that film where Daryl Hannah's a mermaid. For obvious reasons I could never get my head round the mechanics of her lovemaking. I suspect the lights were out and her partner was actually just tossed off by a lobster that owed her a favour. In fairness, Daley's show is just a bit of fun and gives ITV viewers something to do instead of banging on the side of prison vans outside courts trying high-profile cases.

Sir Paul McCartney blasted Stuart Pearce as an 'idiot' for leaving David Beckham out of the final Team GB football squad. Imagine being lectured on team selection by a man who chose Ringo Starr to be in The Beatles and mahogany as a hair colour. I'm surprised Pearce didn't point out who the real idiot was when it came to choosing the right guy: Mark Chapman.

Say what you like about Beckham, but he really has lived the dream – the weird dream in which you've got a voice like a castrated parrot and you're married to a skeleton. Beckham was the highest-paid footballer in Major League Soccer's history. Mind you, the second-highest-paid player was paid in food stamps. Beckham finished his career in Paris. He even learnt some of the language, but when he tried asking for *soixante-neuf* in Paris's red-light district he just ended up with five dozen eggs. Victoria didn't want to move to China as she'd probably have ended up in a jar as a treatment for trapped wind.

Oscar Pistorius and his girlfriend were called the South African Posh and Becks. David, if you're reading this then you know what you have to do next. Nobody who reads about the Oscar Pistorius case does so for a good reason. If you're telling yourself that you follow it because you're interested in how the media respond to it or because of what it says about celebrity you're even worse than the rest of us ghouls. Just be honest about your unsavoury fascination and join us with your popcorn in Modern Hell.

Pistorius was apparently annoyed about having to give up his guns. You can understand his worry. Can you imagine being in a restaurant, going to the toilet and seeing the 'engaged' sign . . . but not being able to shoot the person inside? He held his own personal memorial service for Reeva Steenkamp. Presumably his way of softening the blow before he asked her family if he could have her legs.

Pistorius slept with a baseball bat and a cricket bat, which seems crazy when he's got two false legs. She must have realised he was armed as they're the only limbs he's got. He says he wasn't trying to kill an intruder, just make them eligible for the next Paralympics. The tragedy is that if he had no arms, this would never have happened.

All kinds of records could be set simply by letting him fire the starting pistol at the women's 100 metres. Poor Reeva Steenkamp. Her last moments must've been like a scene from *The Terminator*. Still, a black woman in South Africa could get killed by a disembodied head and not make the papers. Pistorius said when he heard a noise in the bathroom he felt incredibly vulnerable and feared that it was a burglar coming to steal his huge arsenal of guns, rifles and various other weapons. The police found steroids in his house; he must have been on something if he was injecting them into his metal legs.

It seems in South Africa police trying to work out if someone is a murderer use the 'it takes one to know one' policy. In a dramatic turn of events Detective Hilton Botha was dropped from the case as he himself has been charged with seven attempted murders. You know what they say. It takes a thief to catch a thief. What they don't say is that it takes a mass murderer to catch a murderer. Although that's not a bad idea for a new BBC Four drama. Peter Sutcliffe time-travels back to Victorian London to find out who Jack the Ripper is. I'd watch it! The detective has been accused of bungling the investigation. Drugs he claimed were steroids turned out to be a herbal remedy. And the grisly cache of severed limbs he unearthed turned out to be Pistorius's leg drawer.

The murder rate is so high in South Africa that it's not uncommon for at least eight out of the twelve jurors to be convicted murderers. And for the judge to call a halt in proceedings so he can go out and kill. Pistorius has a good chance of getting off because this is his first murder. If he doesn't, his next race will be to try to bagsy the bottom bunk in his prison cell.

• • •

In 2013 we said farewell to Sir Alex Ferguson. The hairdryer. So-called as he'd often give players a terrible shock by jumping in the post-match bath. You mustn't underestimate

Ferguson's skill – to retain the attention of men so highly sexed they don't even draw the line at relatives. The thing is, football is a hobby for most people so what's he going to take up when he retires? A regional manager's position at the Prudential?

David Moyes seems the perfect replacement – he looks like Sir Alex but from a parallel universe where football clubs are managed by six-foot frogs. Ferguson invented the phrase 'squeaky-bum time'. There's been a variety of responses from Man Utd fans, some exclaiming 什么他妈的?!, some leaving offerings of rice at improvised shines, while others simply stared wistfully at the double shadows cast by their binary suns.

Fergie's seventy-one. Though in Scottish years that makes him 120. When he took the job the ground was called New Trafford. He's getting on a bit – he'd reached that age where he'd enter the Champions League and then forget what he'd gone in there for. It's quite difficult to monitor the health of a man who always looks like his liver is using his nose to signal for help.

Ferguson was at Man Utd for so long he's being taught about modern society by the Ohio kidnapping victims. Must be quite strange to look at the world after spending most of your life with football players, to walk blinking on to a high street full of women who aren't crying or running away. The first time he sees a woman without a fake tan he'll probably ask how her leukaemia treatment is going.

When Wayne Rooney said he wanted to retire they just replied, 'The one you've got hanging in the backyard is fine.' In the end he was persuaded to stay at Man Utd. Then again,

Wayne could be persuaded that if he unscrewed his belly button his arse would fall off.

Will Man Utd ever get rid of him? It wouldn't take too much to lure him to another club. Probably just the manager patting his knees and going, 'C'mon, boy!' He could go abroad, although I'm not sure he'd cope with the pressure of learning a first language. He's still impressive with the ball. Especially when you consider he's suppressing the urge to bite it and shake it about till it goes flat. A transfer wouldn't be easy for him to cope with as he's only recently come to terms with Sir Alex trying to explain to him in 2010 that he wasn't his real dad. Wayne's not happy about having to play second fiddle to someone Man Utd have only just bought. Now he knows how Coleen's felt over the years.

The Rooneys have bought a couple of racehorses. They agreed on horses, although initially Wayne was keen to buy a hare, as he'd noticed their repeated success at greyhound stadiums. Coleen's told Wayne he should race their horses next year. But he reckons that's not fair as they've got loads more legs than him. I'd rather see him stick to riding about on his tricycle. The thought of him on horseback is a terrifying portent of the rise of the planet of the apes.

Wayne's been hogging the changing-room mirrors to admire his hair transplant. For the mirror and reflective glass community this is like their 9/11. Still, it's progress. Only six months ago they had to turn it round when he entered so he didn't lash out at 'Bad Wayne who won't stop copying'.

Coleen's had another kid although the couple have had trouble conceiving. My sources tell me it's because Wayne had to break his habit of always withdrawing and ejaculating into a roaring fire in order to destroy DNA evidence.

The Manchester derby was watched by 10 per cent of the global population! Children as far away as Indonesia and El Salvador watched these two great teams play, to make sure they get the stitching on the logos just right. Local derbies always cause resentment, mainly because it's hard for fans to find a post-match prostitute they don't recognise from the school run. A fan in Nairobi was stabbed to death in an argument over the match, presumably by someone who lived on the Salford side of Mount Kenya.

Liverpool player Luis Suárez got a ten-match ban for biting Branislav Ivanovic. I'm using this incident to teach my daughter correct behaviour, which is to always bite an approaching Chelsea player. Being lectured on morals while playing the Chelsea team must be like being told off for farting at a sewage farm.

In fairness to Suárez, having started off with racism it was always going to be tough to find something suitably unpleasant to do next. In many ways biting is his difficult second album. I think the fact that he's being followed by Mike Tyson on Twitter will do him good. He may keep biting but he won't call anyone a n**** again. Suárez was criticised for his behaviour by Graeme Souness. I'd be interested to know how many players would rather have been bitten on the arm by Suárez than booted in the nuts by Souness.

Ivanovic is known for his versatility, going well with chips as well as a light salad. He reacted as any Chelsea player would, by instinctively shouting, 'Not where my wife will see!' Of course, biting is the standard method of tackling in paraplegic football.

It's sad we haven't managed to kick racism out of football. Perhaps we should just try to move it over to table tennis. Still, I don't think we'll go back to the days when football hooliganism was the 'English disease'. It's lost way too much ground to chlamydia.

Paolo Di Canio insisted he isn't a fascist. At least, I think that was the gist of the five-hour speech he gave from his hotel balcony. Apparently, the Sunderland board is thinking of laying down the law to Di Canio. Either renounce your political beliefs or get us a couple of wins against Newcastle. Pull that off on a regular basis and Sunderland would have gladly been run by Fred and Rose West. I'm joking. of course. No one can play at Premier League level with a lumpy pitch.

Di Canio finally denied being a fascist after three days of refusing to talk about his political beliefs. Well, if you'd held the fascist belief that white people are superior then three days in Sunderland should certainly cure you. Although it's hard to look at people in Sunderland without considering that some form of eugenics might not have been a bad idea. It would have been terrible if a fascist had taken over a Premier League football club as they all prefer to keep their ingrained racism on a far more casual level.

Personally, I think that in Roy Hodgson the FA have made a great appointment. Because I'm Scottish. If they hadn't managed to land Hodgson, the FA were going to go for a boiler-suit stuffed full of shredded newspaper with a balloon for a head. Roy struggles to get his tongue round his Rs and I worry it'll impact on team selection. Good news for Walcott, Walker and Welbeck. But Wob Gween's definitely out. If he leaves Rooney on the bench the stadium's likely to turn into that scene from *Life of Brian*. Bwing on . . . you get the idea.

With the next World Cup England just need to focus on the positives that can be achieved. A twenty-three-man squad – that's 4,600 duty-free fags, for starters. How do you make England hungrier for the opponent's goal? Surely rubbing an old pair of knickers on the posts would be a start.

Scotland's chances in the World Cup might be slim but at least we won the Homeless World Cup! A great performance when you consider that in the final they had a man sent off for fighting with himself and one of their players was a dog. Of course, England will be formidable opposition next year once Gazza's eligible, but who would deny these guys their moment of glory? Only their estranged families.

Gazza's out of rehab and he's vowed never to drink again. People say some crazy things when they're pissed, although, to be fair, he does look a lot steadier on his knees. Gazza's flown back, and it's said that the US air marshal who was sitting beside him was worried al-Qaeda might try to bring the plane down by sparking up a Zippo when Gazza burped. The real tragedy of Gazza's situation is why did no one see it coming? Where were the signs? Gazza says he's started having Botox injections. That explains why his forehead's no longer conveying emotion, though not why his eyes and his voice aren't.

It's not fair to say that he's fallen off the wagon. It's more accurate to say that the wagon has been fitted with a fighter plane-style ejector seat and Gazza's pulled the red lever. He wants to be on the next series of *I'm a Celebrity*. When asked about being covered in creepy-crawlies he said he was just praying they would have all gone by then.

My favourite moment was when he confessed he gave a driving examiner £25 to pass his test. Witnesses say it was actually a Snickers wrapper, and he gave it to a butcher who just spun him round a few times and pushed him out of the shop. It seems the instructor had already been won over by Gazza, as when they'd run out of petrol he'd kindly got the car going again by pissing in the petrol tank.

Such a sad decline. Newcastle United, Spurs, Lazio, Rangers . . . now he's only fit for the Scottish First Division. His chances of drying out are currently so low he's been made honorary Mayor of Atlantis.

• • •

A tabloid newspaper investigation last year revealed that a sizeable number of Premier League footballers were taking cocaine. I'd love to see Wayne Rooney doing coke. After a few snorts I imagine the inside of his head would look like the world's bleakest snow globe. I'm against drugs in sport. We can't let children see drug users being athletic; they might realise their parents aren't too wasted to take them to the park.

Frankie Dettori's failed a drugs test for cocaine. The thought of an Italian talking on cocaine is terrifying. He was tested after he did a circuit around a racecourse with a horse on his back. As long as the horse is clean what does it matter what drugs he's on? His job is basically being small, sitting and hanging on. The only substance jockeys should be banned from using is superglue. Anyway, the Grand National is actually part of a conspiracy to produce snuff movies for the centaurs who own our banking system.

Footballers are sharing intimate photos of girls they've slept with. Though in Ched Evans's pics it's hard to tell whether the girl is having sex or planking. These sportsmen have to use BlackBerrys, partly because of the Messenger service and partly because the iPhone's voice control means every time they talk about an arsehole they've just seen it rings Joey Barton. The sex ring was described as 'sleazy' – which is disappointing. I like my sex rings to be wholesome and homespun. People liken football to sex but sex is never that good – who's ever had a miserable time in a nightclub only to bang a couple in, in quick succession, on the way out of the door?

But it's not just footballers who are at it. In the depth of his troubles Tiger Woods claims he seriously considered leaving golf to become a US Navy SEAL. He'd quickly have become one of their top snipers using nothing more than a three-wood. Imagine Osama bin Laden looking out of his window on to what's essentially the world's biggest sand bunker only to see Tiger Woods taking a backswing and then a tiny white projectile getting exponentially larger until, thwack!, it smashed his fucking face off. Navy SEALs are experts in covert operations. Tiger wouldn't have even needed any training. All he'd have had to have done was imagine he was in a strip club and the enemy combatant was his wife.

Maybe golf is just so fucking boring that Woods's behaviour was unavoidable catharsis. Maybe all sport requires so much repetition that some form of sociopathy is inevitable. And most of these guys don't even get to be winners. Most of them are just training to be fast enough to photobomb the back of a shot of Usain Bolt as he goes over the finishing line.

Golf might be boring but it's not as bad as tennis. Lots of people camped outside the entrance to Wimbledon, as that was much more interesting than actually going inside. Wimbledon was first held in 1877 when someone had a glut of strawberries they needed to get rid of. Andy Murray cried after winning the final. It's lovely to see a Scotsman crying where the scene doesn't involve handcuffs, an empty bottle of flavoured vodka and his ex-wife's recently kicked-to-death dog. I'm trying to remember the last time I cried. Coincidentally, it was also the last time I masturbated. To pinpoint it more precisely, it was this evening when *The One Show* did a feature on breast cancer. A British man hadn't won Wimbledon for seventy-seven years but we have to remember that's only because it was seventy-six years ago that people from other countries started playing tennis.

It can't be easy for English people to know that Wimbledon has been won by the first Scotsman ever to pick up a tennis racket. Gerard Butler was there, smiling like somebody had deleted every film he's made since *300* from his IMDb profile. Even Victoria Beckham was smiling, as if she'd just broken out of Arkham Asylum and was about to kill Robin. Having a Scottish tennis champion has certainly given us something big to live up to; we only had the discovery of penicillin and the invention of TV till now.

Andy's been awarded the Freedom of Stirling. That's like on your eighteenth birthday finding out your parents have had a key cut especially for you that opens the bin cupboard. People are calling for him to be knighted because he's done something no other Brit has done for the past seventy-six years. But that could set a precedent. They'd have to knight the next person who was funny on Radio 1 and the next person to finger Susan Boyle.

Andy is set to earn £100 million. If I were in his position I'd buy up every tennis ball in the world, incinerate them and then enjoy my money safe in the knowledge that I'd never have to play that fucking stupid game ever again. For the first few years I'd be celebrating so hard that I'd turn up for every match dressed as a pirate and at the end of every set I'd lay my knob out on the baseline and demand Hawkeye took a picture.

Did you watch the Virgin London Marathon? Anyone who's got Virgin broadband or used their trains will know that a marathon is the quickest way of reaching someone twenty-six miles away. How about those elite runners from Kenya? Their time was a little slower than usual as they were repeatedly stopped and searched by the Metropolitan Police. It's weird to see people running through the streets of London without plasmas. I grew up in a place where if you saw a guy running in a Mickey Mouse costume he was a paedophile. We were sponsoring him to buy a vibrator.

Still, I think my favourite sports story of the year was that Sharran Alexander, the thirty-two-stone, six-foot mum from

West London, is the entire British sumo wrestling team by herself. She's hoping to fight in Japan this month but it depends on funding – and whether they've got biscuits over there. She says there's not much that sportswomen of her size can do – it's pretty much just sumo and allowing pole vaulters to land on you. She's got to be the only top sports star who uses Stacey Soloman as their nutritionist. Apparently, the rest of the sumo team quit but brave Sharran has made sure they haven't been missed, and the food budget remains as high as ever. I'd love to see her *Rocky*-style training montage – 'Eye of the Tiger' ringing out and sweat pouring down her face as she picks up her fourteenth Cherry Bakewell.

7

TV

The best TV show ever would be a programme where really fat people were made to live in a house with a really thin door, and the winner would be whoever got thin enough to get out first. And all the furniture was made of cake. But we can't even have that because it wouldn't be quite deadening enough.

I find it incredibly odd that TV, a terrible succession of images of ever-increasing meanness and bankruptcy, holds such a fascinating appeal for people. Even those like me, who believe they reject it, watch and tweet about it. Maybe we kid ourselves that we're talking about the death of culture or something. Really, we're just sprinkling the salt that helps people shovel this shit into themselves. Sometimes, when I found myself on TV crucifying some celeb or game show, I wondered if I wasn't just filling the role of the 'Two Minutes Hate' in *1984*.

I actually think that being viewed ironically is the only way much of our culture can survive. How could Louis Walsh be viewed with *sincere feeling*? If we view Louis Walsh as a text, there's no reading of him that suggests he is supposed to be interpreted as anything other than the very arseflute we feel so superior about viewing him as.

Indeed, it's possible that sincerity would destroy capitalism, as none of its products are really supposed to inspire sincere feeling. There's a singer called Daniel Johnston, who was a big influence on Nirvana, and a great documentary was made about his mental illness called *The Devil and Daniel Johnston*. At one point he's in an asylum, really struggling, and he asks his manager to try to get him a job writing jingles for Mountain Dew, the fizzy drink. He's an amazing artist who's just obsessed with writing this jingle, for some reason. They play the song he wrote over a shot of the Mountain Dew vending machine in the asylum. It's just this heartbreakingly beautiful thing crafted from love and disappointment and regret and it's all about Mountain Dew. And, of course, it's hard not to sit there and think what a stupid fucking thing Mountain Dew is to sing that about. In the face of his sincerity, the triviality and crassness of cans of sugary water seems obvious. So instead, Mountain Dew get (previously) credible rappers to do ironic promos and there's a general air of 'Hey, we all know what this is, right? This is the bit where I've got to sell you the drink', and it sure sells a lot of fizzy pop.

As a comedian, I find it odd that people imagine a comedian is better because they've seen them on TV. When I see a comic on TV it's . . . well . . . it's kind of like when I see a doctor on TV. Someone good at presenting themselves without necessarily being technically competent. A haircut. A cunt. It's almost fun that something as banal as telly has this hold over people. Like everybody sat down of an evening and stared at a ball of coloured wool. A nurse actually stabbed her boyfriend to death because he didn't want to watch *Harry Hill's TV Burp*. Well, there was only one way to decide . . . FIGHT!

Being a comedian gives you an interesting view of how the media works. Most people whom I've read writing media columns for papers seem barely above the level of punters. I wonder if maybe this is because there's a lot of money in TV, and if you had any understanding of how programmes worked you'd go and make some yourself.

One thing you notice is the increasing depoliticisation of TV shows. Obviously, there's still a huge political agenda at work, but much less overt politics. The main satire show in Britain, *Have I Got News for You*, begins with picture jokes so forced and dispiriting they act as a kind of ideological security scan. If you can smile and nod your way through that shit then they know you won't flip out during the shrieking cognitive dissonance of playing guessing games against a backdrop of worldwide war and financial meltdown.

I was on there once when they showed a picture of a girl being captured by police as she tried to steal a leg of frozen lamb. She was pictured attempting to climb a fence as several police officers dragged her down from below. Everyone made jokes like, you know, maybe she should have stolen three more legs and ridden off on them. I dimly knew I was supposed to join in with a 'I suppose if you saw enough lamb thieves jumping over a fence you'd fall asleep!' or whatever, but all I could think was how hungry do you have to be to steal a leg of frozen lamb. I can't imagine what any decent human being could possibly have interjected. 'She looks frightened', perhaps.

There's always a terror on these shows that someone will say something offensive, but there's a bigger fear of someone saying something relevant. In a world where we fly remote-control bombs into civilians and rip out our planet's lungs to fund our appetite for shiny gee-gaws, I find the idea of being offended at a joke vaguely decadent. I don't wish any harm on such people, except perhaps that they suddenly develop a sense of irony as they tweet their moral outrage on a phone made by a suicidal slave.

I think if someone announced that the whole of the last couple of decades of telly had actually been a huge overarching art project about banality and worthlessness, a deliberately clumsy shadow play of exhausted memes, I would stand up and applaud. Perhaps you can just view it that way, anyway. I mean, the only interpretation that really matters for you is your own. I always enjoy *The Matrix* a lot more by pretending that Morpheus is the spiritually enlightened version of Laurence Fishburne's character in *King of New York*.*

Perhaps our media output is an enormous subconscious defence mechanism. You know how radio waves and TV signals travel off through space? Perhaps we know that we're not ready for first contact and fear the malevolence of a race

* Also, my reading is that Peter Pan and the Lost Boys are the souls of abortions. It would certainly explain Captain Hook.

advanced enough to travel easily among the stars. So that's what our culture is for. No technocratic alien race will willingly visit the world that produces *Take Me Out*.

Look at the sheer creative morbidity of our top-rating shows. *Strictly* gets 11.5 million viewers – I never even realised there were so many people in the country going through the menopause. The show lost viewers with Bruce's return – which shocked me. I thought the only point in watching was the grim anticipation of seeing him collapse, develop a cocoon, then fly off like a giant moth.

Alan Sugar says that *The Apprentice* has not been sexed-up for ratings. It must be for more sinister reasons, then. It was the sexiest series so far, yet still presented by a man who looks like he's been cleaned out of someone's belly button.

I have to accept some responsibility for *The X Factor*'s reappearance this year. The sloppy calibration of my flux capacitor meant I failed to go back to 1924 as planned, and beat John Logie Baird to death with a replica *TV Quick* Best Entertainment Show Award. I overshot by a full decade, the one consolation being that, thanks to my efforts, we've at least been spared the empty hypnotic indulgence of Professor Hugo Moffat's clockwork mesmetron.

I confess I lost a big *X Factor* bet at the bookies this time round. I'd got 4 to 1 on me taking my own life before the end of the series. Every week we've heard who was the bookies' favourite. Is that much of a guide? Can the best judge of the nation's mainstream musical tastes really be someone whose perfect sound is a chorus of divorced men coughing and sobbing as they try to light tear-stained roll-ups?

In 2012 *The X Factor* lost two million viewers. Perhaps it's simply becoming harder to operate a remote control when you've got cloven hooves and a twitch. I think 'viewers' is the wrong word. It's too active. Still, I suppose there's just not the space to write 'This Saturday two million fewer people had the deluded shuffling of sterile karaoke puppets reflected in the glaze that coats their lifeless eyes.' I've started to wonder whether ratings are down because people have absorbed all the crap they can take. Maybe it's literally brimming up to their eyeballs and when they next chop an onion their face will shit itself. Are there too many ad breaks on it now? I'm glad of them. At least it's a relative break from the relentless commercialism.

But these declining viewing figures are a concern. Experts estimate if they don't stop falling, by 2032 the show will be forced to travel door-to-door, contestants trying to win viewers over by singing through their letterboxes. It will constitute a sorry procession, forced to trundle its way from town to town in cages set upon little wooden carts, Simon's brain atop in a nutrient-filled jar, the whole affair pulled along by a team of blinded stray dogs, relentlessly driven forward by a cackling hooded driver dangling an Asda Smart Price sausage from a fishing rod.

I'm enjoying the *X Factor* iPhone app where you can hit a button to clap or boo the acts. To get a rat in a lab to do that they'd have to give it some kind of reward – perhaps by making the singing stop. A lot of the show seems to involve cutting back to the judges' faces as they run through the three or four emotions available to them. Except Louis, who always has the startled look of a sleeping pensioner who's just heard a noise downstairs.

Louis always says 'You deserve to be on that stage' to everyone he sees, when realistically that would only be true if he were standing in front of a gallows. Simon needs to find a way of getting better judges on the show – perhaps with some sort of televised judging contest. Gary Barlow's performance is utterly compelling. His voice has a faraway, hollow quality, as if during a séance his body's been seized by some blasphemous entity. I keep expecting him to interrupt someone covering 'Valerie' with a haunting monologue about the indignities his soul is suffering in hell. Perhaps his ghost can only rest if he uses boot camp to get the bands to solve his own murder. When the triumphant spirit explodes as incandescent light from a screaming Gary's nose, mouth and eyes, we can all tap the clap button.

I'm surprised Britney Spears managed to get a job on the US *X Factor*. The last time she went near a judging panel they took her kids away. Britney is pumping weights, and doing yoga and kick-boxing. She will soon hold the title of fittest woman alive that no one wants to fuck. Her fans vented their anger about her lacklustre UK shows. I saw a bit of Britney's dance routines on the news – in fairness, I thought I was watching Libyan rebels dispose of Gaddafi's corpse. It's hardly surprised that Britney doesn't look totally focused – in fairness, she's probably trying to work out where she is, who she is and why a voice is telling her to kill. I wonder why famous people even get mental disorders. What tips them over the edge from their usual happy setting of just wanting the whole world to worship them?

Nicole Scherzinger says she's been feeling lonely since her split from Lewis Hamilton. She confessed that she has no friends in London and has been reduced to dining out with her own staff – as if they were real human beings! Nicole had to fork out thousands for a flight upgrade after *X Factor* bosses booked her into economy. Luckily, she could put it on her card. If she'd had to busk for it in departures she'd still be there when plate tectonics had solved the problem. Of course, these days former *X Factor* winner Steve Brookstein travels for free. Simon's had his skin made into a natty set of matching luggage. To this day he swears that when he opens the shoulder bag he sometimes hears a plaintive 'We'll make another album soon, won't we Si?' drifting up from features a casual glance might assume were just blemishes in the leather.

You remember Steve Brookstein? 'What's the time?' 'Steve Brookstein time.' That one.

I had my fingers crossed that James Arthur would win *The X Factor*, so that we'd never hear of him again. Do be careful, James. It appears that Simon's tucked a clause in your contract that should your album flop he can hang your ornately inked pelt from the wall of his walk-in humidor. Fans queued overnight to meet James. I'd queue up overnight to see him, the same way I would have done if I'd been alive in Victorian times and had the chance to see Joseph Merrick, the Elephant Man. James can now enjoy what being an *X Factor* winner means. Constant Twitter abuse, one failed album and a brief part in a shit West End musical. James said, 'I'm probably going to get my teeth fixed. It's not a vanity thing.' Well, it is, and it will be like putting twenty-six-inch rims on a wheelie bin.

Fellow *X Factor* champions Little Mix say they're bidding to crack America. Shouldn't they start by trying to crack Britain first? Little Mix show just how little you can achieve without any talent or hard work. Little Mix. Less a band name, more a description of the group's gene pool. They look so young I just don't feel comfortable playing the usual girl-band 'In which order would you?' game. OK, if you insist. I suppose I'd behead the blonde one first, then beat the other three to death with her corpse. The girls are proud to say they're teetotal and never touch drugs. They get high on life! And suffer from a desperate addiction to the approval of total strangers. They want to inspire their fans. Good! About time little girls had some proper role models. I can't be the only parent getting fed up of all that 'I want to be a vet, I want to be a nurse' bullshit.

Presumably the first inspirational message of empowerment for their legion of young fans will be, 'Yes, you too can endorse goods or products as directed by your management.' Simon wants them to focus on the music. Apparently, in their contract he's even decreed their vaginas be covered in hot wax before receiving the seal of his holy ring.

Clean-living Little Mix have adopted 'We won't steal your boyfriend' as their motto. It's a self-help mantra that's been used unsuccessfully by the members of Westlife, Boyzone and in the adapted form, 'I won't steal your boy', by none other than Michael Jackson. They've been described as so likeable they could sell coals to Newcastle. That expression should be updated – how about, 'They could sell a Federico Fellini boxed set in Newcastle'?

The girls were slammed for using an autocue. An autocue machine, yes, like they have down those autocue bars where hen nights sing 'I Will Survive'. I hear that they were told not to learn the lyrics to their songs as Simon considers it essential to dull the winners' powers of recall, so family and past friends don't hinder reprogramming.

Sharon Osbourne returned to the UK to be an *X Factor* judge, confirmation apparently coming when a deserted ship, the long-dead skipper lashed to the wheel and the hold containing just a single chest freezer, bumped eerily into a jetty at Southampton. Her return means that Sharon and Ozzy Osbourne are living apart. They've stayed together through thick and thin – or Jack and Kelly, as they're otherwise known.

They wanted to inject something new into the show so they've brought back Sharon – who, of course, has had so many new things injected into her you could bounce a coin off her face. Sharon's set to do *X Factor* mentoring by Skype. Is Skyping right for an *X Factor* judge? Maybe I'm tiring of the show but the way I'd most like to see them giving advice is via an Ouija board. Contestants mustn't worry, as they can ask Simon's advice at any point, just by writing their question in urine dribbled from an upturned crucifix, then throwing it into the fire. The great thing about Sharon is that she speaks her mind – it's just a pity that her mind appears to be haunted by the soul of an angry dockworker. Personally, I've missed Sharon's little words of wisdom – to make up for it I've had to spike my nan's tea with meths. I was sad that Tulisa's been given the heave-ho. I liked Tulisa on there – with her boobs and hairy Greek arms you could squint and imagine Simon was still there.

Simon says he's a workaholic; judging by his face, so's his plastic surgeon. Simon looks like he's had the Botox applied by someone whose only qualification is a three-week upholstery course they took in prison. On the plus side for Simon, at least his hair's no longer the weirdest looking thing on his head.

What about that Simon Cowell biography by Tom Bower? It described the life of a tortured genius. Perhaps a slight over-statement, though I'd do anything to make that phrase just half true. He's had so many affairs! Simon managed to keep them secret by only ever having sex with all these women in the privacy of his publicist's imagination. The author had access to Simon's entire inner circle – mainly soft toys who've attained a level of higher trust by having their button eyes removed. The book costs £18.99. Though if you sent me £9.99 I'll gladly send you my summary in an old Pringles tube.

Simon wasn't available for further comment. He's believed to be in an aircraft hanger full of tenners somewhere, a leaf blower in each hand, gleefully shrieking beyond the audible human spectrum. And in a desperate search for scandal, hidden cameras have been installed in all the *X Factor* back-stage rooms. This shit running for eight years isn't considered scandal enough.

It seems that Simon was 'feeling very low' over the rev-elations about his private life, according to a press release to promote the revelations about his private life. A lot of girls Simon has slept with are coming out of the woodwork. Well, from the look of them they're coming out of the waxworks. I don't believe it he did it eleven times in one night – glamour model Alicia Douvall just doesn't look like that sort of woman, the type that can count. I'll bet Simon can, if the guy is hot enough. I'm joking – I really mean, if the guys are hot enough. I'm joking – I really mean, if they guys are paid enough. I'm joking – I really mean, if the guys are finished in the recording studio. Only kidding. Simon's said he doesn't care if people think he's gay as it's nothing to be ashamed of. Not true, Simon. If it turned out you were gay the homosexual community would be extremely ashamed.

Yes, in Bower's book the cat is out of the bag. Simon's a tiger in the sack. He's ruined more springs than a Scottish weatherman. The book says he tried to shag Cheryl, but she told him she didn't want to spoil the happiness she'd found. She was dying of malaria at the time. These endless stories about Simon being unlucky in love are his best chance of looking human since he stopped living with a professional make-up artist. You can't make Simon seem human! I've got more chance of sympathising with a dry-stone wall that falls on a toddler.

Simon's been likened to a Roman emperor – how times have changed. While Nero had the power to end a gladiator's life, Simon orders the mentally challenged to sing 'Mama Do the Hump' while their leggings sag around their arse. Dannii Minogue had an affair with Simon. Now we know why she spells her first name that way; she wants to distance herself as much as possible from the reality of who she is. He said, 'It was her sexy clothes and tits – it was genuine love.'

Remind me, in which of Shakespeare's love sonnets does he compliment a lady's clothes and tits again?

No wonder Dannii went from Simon to a rugby player. Once she'd bought the strap-on, she may as well use up its warranty. Dannii went to Twitter to ask for privacy, displaying the same logic as when she turned to Simon for love. Resorting to Twitter to ask for privacy is a bit like asking a zombie horde for a vegetarian gravy recipe. It's said Simon liked to treat the female judges like 'toys' – presumably, then, Dannii was a doll who's face has been repaired and Sharon was one that was used too much by rough kids then left in a carrier bag out the front of Oxfam.

Simon's got a woman – Lauren Silverman – pregnant. It seems the conception was touch and go, Lauren almost regaining consciousness halfway through as she'd only eaten half the chocolate mousse. Simon claims he never wanted children. Which, to be honest, is probably the best thing to say when you're in the music industry and Operation Yewtree are buzzing about. It's the age-old story – millionaire flat-topped androgyne impregnates property mogul's wife on ocean-going yacht. The woman's husband must be gutted – after all, he only invited Simon on holiday so he could use his man-tits as a travel pillow. It's Sinitta who I feel sorry for – if she doesn't play nice with the new baby she'll be put in a cattery.

I think he'll be a good dad – surely there's no way he's able to sleep at night anyway. He likes the idea of being a dad. Of course he does. Who doesn't like the idea of being a dad? Even women like the idea of being a dad. Never having to do the night feeds. Taking a week off work and then never really having to spend any time with the kid until it's seven. Being a dad is great.

Except, of course, when it isn't. When all you want is to be as far away from your offspring as possible. That's why they're called 'offspring', because most of the time you'd like to go off without your children and come back sometime around spring.

Then again, Simon has the money to make it work. As dads, which one of us hasn't at some point wanted to turn our backs on the kid and climb into a helicopter, and, as it hovers above our home with a bearing set for the south of France, shower the nannies with £20 notes while shouting over the noise of the rotors, 'Good luck, Consuela; the little fucker's your problem – see you next spring'?

Simon hasn't the patience to sit through fifteen seconds of a ventriloquist's act. How's he ever going to deal with a toddler saying 'toast' repeatedly for four hours? People in Simon's circle said the pregnancy seemed very out of character. Which is an understated way of saying, 'HOLY SHITBALLS! THIS AIN'T RIGHT! THE GUY'S MORE BENT THAN THE ZIMBABWEAN ELECTIONS!!'

• • •

I always wonder why, on *Britain's Got Talent*, they cut back to Amanda Holden for reactions? Her face doesn't fucking move! They might as well cut to *V for Vendetta*, or that crystal skull Arthur C. Clarke was always banging on about.

I honestly don't know if there's more poison in Simon's heart or Holden's forehead. The reason Amanda Holden gets so many Botox jabs into her forehead is to prevent all the worry lines that would result from trying to work out how shagging Les Dennis fifteen years ago qualifies her to judge a talent contest. If Holden cries any more then I'm worried the salt water will warp whatever it is her face is made out of. Mind you, Simon's face now looks puffier than the Puffa jacket that Puff Daddy would wear on a puffin-watching trip.

Half a million pounds for the winner – *Britain's Got Talent* is the only place left in the country where the mentally disabled actually get some money. This year they opened the series in the contestants' houses to explain why they're auditioning. How are they going to top that next year? Go back one step further and explain it by showing the contestants' mothers downing vodka in pregnancy? It must be a weird job for David Walliams, slowly realising that every character he's created has been surprisingly sane and realistic.

After a fourteen-year-old boy with cerebral palsy did a stand-up routine, Alesha Dixon said, 'You were great. You made me laugh before the act even started.' Good one, Alesha – and people said you were just a face on a stick.

Saudi Arabia's version of the show, *Buraydah's Got Talent*, isn't going to allow singing, dancing or women. It sounds restrictive, but technically Subo could still have won it. I can't wait for the Saudi Simon Cowell – a controlling, power-hungry man with a dislike of women.

Thailand's Got Talent went the other way and shocked viewers with a contestant who paints using her breasts, something I've tried with my partner to spice things up in the bedroom. Way more trouble than it was worth, so we switched to rollers for the lounge. It's double standards. This woman paints with her tits and gets worldwide recognition, yet when Susan Boyle does it she gets tasered outside her local chip shop and charged with graffiti.

I was sad that ITV and the BBC decided to schedule *The Voice* and *Britain's Got Talent* against each other, because I was worried that I might finally run out of hate. I suppose it's not a big deal because we've all got hard-disc recorders now. If they're both on at the same time you can just watch something good you taped earlier that week.

If it weren't for *The Voice* then judges like Danny Wotsit would be nobodies today. It's the show where the judges turn their backs on the contestants. A bit like *The X Factor* a week or two after the final. If they want music-industry realism surely they should have it so contestants perform with the judges only being able to see the top of their heads.

Not being able to see contestants is an interesting format tweak. If they can just eliminate the other four senses, too, they'll have really nailed it. Not looking directly at contestants is hardly original. Even now when Simon has a meeting with Susan Boyle I hear he reverses up to her using the reflection in the back of his highly polished shield.

People get snobby about watching *The Voice* and say, 'Oh, I want to see REAL singers.' Go out, then! Go out! You're watching a reality show where the judges have been picked purely on their ability to grunt in slightly different ways. Danny O'Donoghue said he needed coaching to stop himself swearing on the show. I just have one thing to say about that. Who the fuck's Danny O'Donoghue? Whoever he is, he has a brutal 80s flat-top. Like Skynet built a special Terminator to infiltrate Cork's gay community. I think there should be another celebrity on the back of the chair and the chair should keep spinning really fast, so they kind of strobe into a single entity. What a thrill for contestants to have their career ended by a hybrid of Christina Aguilera and Mr. T, who has never even seen their face.

Jessie J looks like someone has pitched the elixir of youth on *Dragons' Den* and didn't mention it had side effects. Bless Jessie for getting her head shaved for charity; but she's afflicted with a bit of a man-face – she now looks like Action Man has moulted. I believe her when she says it's 'not about the money', so she must be a judge on *The Voice* because she genuinely hates music. But it does need that Susan Boyle moment, doesn't it? Someone hitting a note so high that the rest of will.i.am's hair pops out of his head.

Viewing figures for *The Voice* started high and then dwindled after they stopped the spinning chairs. To combat this, next series they're going to keep Jessie J in a centrifuge machine like an inarticulate tranny kaleidoscope. Of course, being on *The Voice* did wonders for the career of its first winner, Leanne Mitchell – mainly because she now works in MFI as a revolving-chair saleswoman.

I don't need to watch people recruiting young women on to a 'team' without having seen their real faces – that's just an evening on Twitter for me. Viewers liked it when the judges couldn't see the acts, so they're going to speed through the singing and finish the series with a close-up of Tom's cataracts slowly taking hold. Tom rarely gets all of his favourite singers on his team, as he kept accidentally pressing the large red button on his emergency necklace.

The 'battle' round is always very exciting. Last year I watched a fat bloke in a Hawaiian shirt scream 'Sign, Sealed, Delivered I'm Yours' into a middle-aged dinner-lady's face and I've never felt more alive.

• • •

The BBC had high hopes that *The Voice* would put it back on the map in the face of ITV's dominance of the reality TV space. But for the BBC to flourish it needs its biggest supporters to get behind it. Maybe it's time to accept we'll just have to sell it to a group of wealthy paedophiles. Yes, it's radical, but they'd only have to paint over the bottom bit of that first 'B'. Toilet signs were among hundreds of items pilfered by souvenir hunters after BBC TV Centre's final broadcast, as people filled their houses with objects covered in paedo DNA.

Vernon Kaye was escorted out of the BBC when security caught him trying to steal a dressing-room sign. At least, that's the reason they gave him. You didn't need that sign, Vernon, you've been stealing from the BBC your whole career. I took a lifesize model of George Alagiah, which I keep in my wardrobe. But it's started to make knocking and sobbing noises so I might have to chuck it out.

George Entwistle resigned as director general. He'd only been in the job for fifty-four days. To be fair, I've been in jobs longer than that and still not known where the toilets are. It must have been an awkward leaving do to arrange. I don't think they do cakes in Patisserie Valerie that say, 'Sorry, you got the paedophile wrong.' Trust has been lost in the BBC now. To be honest, I thought that it was lost after the first series of *The One Show*.

The BBC's sloppiness reflects badly on all journalists. Not least tabloid ones, as when trawling the internet for stories they often end up copying and pasting from bbc.co.uk.

Tell you who you don't hear much from lately – that woman who insisted she was the illegitimate child of Jimmy Savile. It seems that almost every day for a couple of years a new, well-known face is unveiled in the relentless Advent calendar of sexual abuse. I, for one, look forward to the mass trial of Britain's celebrities at some paedophile Nuremberg. Honestly, the way things are going, I wouldn't be surprised if I heard that Dave Benson Phillips used to wank into the gunge tank. I was never into the celebrity paedo parties. I'd stand in the corner and simulate the experience by having Jeremy Beadle give me a handjob. Once, Mike Reid gave me a Reacharound.

When I heard Rolf Harris had been arrested I thought it was for his performance at the Royal Jubilee. If Rolf goes on trial then at least the courtroom artist won't feel under any pressure to do a good job. They'll probably find it hard to resist drawing him with the body of a kangaroo.

The owner of the first time-machine will have a moral dilemma about whether to kill Hitler or bomb the 1988 Royal Variety Performance. It seems when it comes to TV, the author L. P. Hartley was right: the past is a foreign country.

Paedoslovakia. Ironically, the only non-paedophile on telly in the 80s was Ian Krankie. Perhaps evidence will emerge that Britain itself is a paedophilic landmass and when we're all drunk at Christmas, it rams Anglesey up Ireland's arse.

Footage emerged of Savile defending Gary Glitter. So, he might have been a predatory paedophile but at least he wasn't a hypocrite. The pair actually invented the platform shoe together, purely as a way of seeing children who were slightly further away.

For those conspiracy theorists who say these scandals will one day be shown to involve our politicians, well, who knows? They kill kids, so there's no reason to think that they wouldn't be fucking them. There are quite feasibly politicians alive today who took to fucking kids just to try to give themselves the stomach required for the real business of government.

The *Sun*'s front page reported 'Gary Glitter's 10 hour sex quiz'. Finally, a show you could imagine Justin Lee Collins hosting. I have to say, Glitter didn't do himself any favours when questioned over child sex offences by trying to bribe police with Top Trumps cards and a Kinder Egg. Officers aren't expected to question him again for a while. As it'll take them months to chip open his laptop with a toffee hammer. Savile's cottage in the Highlands was vandalised. It appears that they've scraped off so many of the hundreds and thousands you can now see the gingerbread walls beneath. Jim Davidson said, 'The Jimmy Savile witch hunt is going a bit silly.' It's not a witch hunt, Jim. Remember, witches never existed.

Jim Davidson was cleared of historic allegations that he sexually molested two women. He says he's 'a gentleman' who once gave up his bed for a drunk dancer. 'I never laid a finger on her, even though she was completely comatose and wouldn't have had a clue what was going on.' I always thought a gentleman 'never tells' but it appears that a gentleman is someone who could have raped someone but didn't.

Davidson says he's not a Jimmy Savile figure. True. People used to like Jimmy Savile.

Davidson was once voted Britain's funniest man. I can understand this, as when I first heard the news of his arrest I couldn't stop laughing. He's previously had brushes with the law after he was banned from driving following a speeding offence. If I were the judge I'd let him keep driving. But ban him from using his seatbelt or his brakes. When he was caught by police and asked if he was the driver he said, 'Can I nominate someone I don't like?' Good luck pinning three points on the entire Pakistani population of the UK. Jim, if the system really allowed us to nominate someone we didn't like you'd currently have two and a half million points on your licence.

I must say Stuart Hall does look very sad. Either he feels guilty or he used up all his laughter in the 70s. Stuart began his career on *Look North*. Unfortunately, while you were looking north he'd be going south. Stuart Hall had a room set aside at the BBC where he could entertain 'lady friends'. No wonder he always appeared animated and excited on screen. He knew he was only seconds away from heading back to his whore-filled room.

Hall got fifteen months. The judge couldn't have given him fifteen years because there was a worry he'd ejaculate on hearing his sentence. He said there was a vendetta against famous people. Hey, if you don't want a vendetta against you, maybe don't abuse so many people they can form a mob. As he was sentenced his victims cried, but he showed no emotion; arousal doesn't reach an eighty-three-year-old's face for a good ten minutes. The sentence was lenient because he had to be tried under the 1956 Act. Shame he didn't have consensual sex with a man. We could have thrown the book at him.

When I think about 70s television one of my major memories is that test-card girl who used to sit really still for hours on end playing noughts and crosses with the clown puppet. Looking back, I think she sat there all night on her own because she was too scared to return to the BBC dressing rooms. You begin to look back at these shows in a different way, now. Was Mr Benn constantly changing outfits just to evade capture from the police? One minute dressed as a Native American, the next as an astronaut, simply to make it harder for his victims to pick him out of a line-up?

Making nostalgia programmes is going to be tricky now. *I Remember the 70s* will just be full of people crying, with a helpline number at the end. People of my age can't look back on the 70s with any enjoyment. At least teenagers nowadays can look back at an innocent world of kids' presenters going on coke binges and hanging themselves. A lot of the guys from the 70s are saying, 'We didn't ask the girls' ages.' To be fair, the fact she's telling you about her pets and her favourite princess means you don't really have to.

With all the scandals, everyone involved in *Children in Need* must be walking on eggshells. Or sitting in a bath of beans. Whichever raises the most money, I guess. They're not even allowed to hold any big cheques anymore in case behind one someone is being sucked off by a teenager. Jimmy Savile was banned from *Children in Need*. Which is lucky, as no one would want to see Pudsey using himself to show the cops where Jimmy touched him.

I must say, I prefer the old *Blue Peter* appeals. There was one for stamps when I was a little boy. There'd been a famine in Ethiopia, and the great thing was, once the target had been reached they kept the viewers involved by sending the presenters out to show the work of the appeal. I remember they took a jumbo from London to Addis Ababa, then a little propeller plane that landed on an airstrip where the forest had been cleared. Then into a Jeep for a day and a half, with the last twenty miles on foot. I can still recall them now, arriving in this simple of village of mud huts and being met by the grateful chief, who took them into his own hut, which was a little larger, the doorway topped with the feathers from colourful birds. You know something? I think he had the biggest stamp collection I've ever seen. There's nothing like a hobby to take your mind off your appetite.

• • •

Ricky Gervais was cleared of breaking Ofcom rules for calling Susan Boyle a 'fucking mong'. Quite right, too. Sometimes a joke has such skill in its construction, such heights of imagination and poetry, that it transcends our petty linguistic taboos. I read a columnist describe him as a moron for saying it and adding that she didn't need to explain why she could use the word 'moron' and he couldn't use 'mong'. Because that's where our culture is at in terms of debate – a kind of secondary-school level.

You'd imagine why someone could use one word rather than another would be the starting point of an undergraduate seminar. Perhaps we would even ask whether meaning is constructed in the listener (phenomenology), or whether the newspapers that publicised Gervais's foolishness were authors by relocation. You know, the idea that if I project a porno on to the front of a local nursery school they arrest me rather than Ron Jeremy. Perhaps most of all we would wonder why modern liberals have a set of words they feel must not be used *regardless of context*. Something you'd normally associate with fundamentalist religion. Instead, we've an increasingly infantilising cultural climate of *because that's just why*.

It seems strange that nobody ever mentions that the ideas of *I want to see interesting, free comedy that pushes boundaries* and *I never want hear a joke I disagree with* are mutually exclusive. Here's an amusing email my agent got recently:

SCOTLAND'S JESUS

Hi Hannah

I write a column for the **** ******.

I was concerned to read in the Sun what Frankie Boyle had written about the death of Brian Cobby, best known as the voice of the speaking clock, saying how he had died 'after his third stroke'.

My understanding is that Mr Cobby did indeed die of a stroke but this seems to me distasteful in any case. I would like a comment from Boyle justifying what he has said and possibly an apology to Mr Cobby's family.

Thanks, *****

•   •   •

People who say you don't see white dog shit anymore haven't been watching *Jeremy Kyle*. Jeremy says he has nothing to lose by doing a quiz show because he's already the most hated man in Britain. That's a level of self-awareness people will never have thought he had and he'll have gone up in their estimation. Although he's still the most hated man in Britain. Kyle's studios have been fitted with walk-through metal detectors. I hope that sends out a clear message to anyone going – 'Remember, you can still punch him.'

Somewhere Angelina Jolie's pre-cancerous boobs are fighting Jeremy's cancer-ridden testicle in the ultimate battle of good vs evil. I was saddened by the news of Jeremy's illness, as I was so close to fully disposing of any residual belief from my Catholic upbringing of an interventionist God. Jeremy wanted the results given to him straight. A shame – really, doctors should have made him wait for three minutes while a bingo-fixated cartoon fox tried to trick him into borrowing money at 1,000 per cent APR. But all respect to Jeremy. It takes some skill to turn abusing street drinkers into a winning format.

Cancer doesn't discriminate, which actually makes it morally superior to Jeremy Kyle. Must've been quite humbling for cancer to enter Jeremy's body and find it's the least toxic substance in there. Like Ian Huntley turning up at a party only to find its Josef Mengele's house. Jeremy won't let cancer beat him! He's never been stopped by lack of talent or conscience, so why stop now? His fans have sent cards. Must be touching to receive a 'Get Well Soon!' card from people who'd spit at a fat person. Having just one testicle shouldn't affect sperm production. A relief for Jeremy, as his pre-show dressing-room ritual consists of ejaculating onto a sculpture of his own face carved from the frozen tears of former guests.

Really, the majority of our TV output is just a kind of sewer of the collective unconscious. On the day of Amanda Knox's trial Matthew Wright's show on Channel 5, *The Wright Stuff*, held a phone-in titled 'Foxy Knoxy: Would Ya?' It couldn't really have been in any worse taste if they'd have gone for 'Fred and Rosemary West: I Don't Fancy Yours Much'. Channel 5 insists the discussion was handled sensitively, and how couldn't it have been when the panel included Christopher

Biggins? It reminded me of the time when Matthew Wright discussed the problem of female circumcision with Lion-O from *ThunderCats*. Matthew knows a sexy murder when he sees one! He realises it would be almost impossible for his viewers to knock one out to the story of a burglar being strangled in Aldershot. And the 'almost' in that sentence must really depress him.

8

ANIMALS

I love the idea of animals being just like, or even superior to, humans but when you really look at it they just seem unable to do very much. Even the worst human doesn't eat off the floor. Indeed, if an animal could rise to the worst of human behaviour it would be a startling achievement. Imagine a pony drugged and raped a young woman in a Travelodge. It would become an international celebrity.

For many people a love of animals is simply a last resort. Animals are at least something that can bear to be around you, admittedly because they don't know how to get food.

We shouldn't get too conceited, however. We might think that our technological achievements mean we transcend animals, but we're not using them to transcend anything. We're using them to eat way too much cheese and broadcast interviews with Bon Jovi.

In many ways pets are more like mirrors – things to project our emotions on to, which makes them feel bored, angry and horny, and annoyed that they have to finish writing their book. We are the descendants of people who kept dogs. The dog's sense of smell was an evolutionary advantage to early society, so that's who we are: the people who wiped out everybody sensible on earth, all the decent people who didn't want to live in a camp covered in shit.

• • •

A fire destroyed the tropical house at Five Sisters Zoo up here in West Lothian. A tropical house in a Scottish zoo? At least the animals would have blissfully croaked 'Thank God' as the heat and flames consumed them. They don't know how it started. My money is on two stick insects shagging.

At Edinburgh Zoo giant pandas Sunshine and Sweetie were filmed attempting to mate. Their keepers got the film off Sunshine's mobile phone. It could be they're just so used to being filmed while mating that Sunshine always feels he has to cum on her tits. Mating is tough because the females only ovulate once a year – although that does mean Mr Panda can go the other eleven months without coming home to her crying because he didn't switch the dishwasher on.

Every year Sweetie only has a day and a half in which to conceive, although a preference for mating in the summer means in a Scottish zoo that window could drop to just eighteen hours. Thirty-six hours to have as much sex as possible – I'd suggest packing them off to a Club 18-30 resort in

Faliraki, sharpish. And hope Sunshine's muscular paws will be able to pull all the Terrys and Daves off Sweetie so he can get a go, too. Of course, there's a chance that Sunshine wasn't making repeated attempts at hugs; he might have been just trying to find Sweetie's zip so he could put away his pyjamas.

London Zoo's tigers have been given a new enclosure to help them breed. It must be great having sex if you're a tiger – when they get to go on top it'll be like doing it on a great big fireside rug. When in season tigers mate ten times a day. I'm told the action's been so hot that even the panda in the next enclosure's started wanking.

BBC One show *Frozen Planet* was accused of fakery because they filmed a polar bear giving birth in a zoo. Of course it wasn't in the Arctic – the only time David Attenborough goes somewhere that cold is when they place him in a carbonite freezer in between series. MP John Whittingdale described it as 'hugely disappointing' – unlike hearing that an MP is spending his time moaning about wildlife shows during the biggest global recession in recent history. TV definitely fakes stuff more than newspapers, a source close to TV said. A friend of Attenborough agreed: 'TV fakes stuff, but newspapers are great', said the unnamed source.

And in another case of unnecessary human intervention in the animal world, a woman in Norfolk has taught a chicken to count. That was nice of her; now it knows exactly how many days left till it gets strangled for Christmas. A quarter of pet owners will share Christmas dinner with their pet. Me too. Lobsters may not be that affectionate, but you try getting your cat to pull a cracker.

There's been a lot of sad news in the animal world recently. Lonesome George the Galapagos turtle died at one hundred years old. The First World War, the Russian Revolution, Hiroshima . . . it's incredible to think of all the things he must have been completely oblivious to. A record breaker even in death, he's now the world's largest ashtray.

We lost another record-breaking animal when the world's biggest boa constrictor was killed after attacking a man in Florida. Boas pair up for life – on hearing the news the dead snake's partner took her own life in a joint suicide pact with a severely depressed porcupine, a further tragedy being that because of the therapeutic power of acupuncture, at the start of her final clench she actually felt just a little bit better.

More bad news. The last known rhinoceroses in Mozambique have been wiped out by poachers. Their horns are prized in Asia for their aphrodisiac and cancer-curing properties. Well, which is it? Surely that could be dangerous, giving a patient with late-stage cancer an unwanted erection for the rest of his life. It costs $100,000 to hunt a rhino in Africa. I'd never do that. I hate flying. But I'm interested to know how much it costs to hunt a rhino in Manchester. I'd do it on a BMX wearing a ski mask. Once it was dead I'd sell its horn as a bong.

American hunters and their families are also paying up to £10,000 for giraffe-hunting expeditions. Ah, shooting giraffes – the American pastime for those whose aim isn't accurate enough to piss on a dead Arab. (I couldn't enjoy watching TV with the head of a dead animal looking at me, which is why I've not been able to follow *It's All About Amy* on Channel 5.)

It's especially sad, as not only do giraffes form an essential part of the savannah ecosystem, but the chimps use them as slides in their theme parks.

Of course, the Africans put up with all this – when they see a white American getting off a plane bristling with guns they're bloody relieved all he wants to do is shoot wildlife. Shooting something twenty-foot tall on a plain actually sounds easier than shooting fish in a barrel.

Having seen the photos of these hunts, my first question is why do hunters wear camouflage? Are the giraffes prone to shooting back at them? It's good for the kids to have these photographs – in later life, simply showing them to their therapists will save a lot of time. If you're a big enough prick to want your kids to have a similar experience but can't afford a flight to Africa, then why not take your toddler to your local petting zoo and spit at the goats?

• • •

A huge badger cull has been given the go-ahead in England. The badgers infect dairy cows with TB. It's a real problem, as too much coughing means their output is then only fit for milk shakes. Step one of the cull will be to gas the badgers' setts. Step two, to check for hidden rooms in the attics of rats and moles. I've a special connection with these animals as I once removed a thorn from a badger's paw. Four times, in fact. In the end I just sacked him and hired a human gardener. Clarissa Dickson Wright has suggested that we eat the badgers that are being culled. This shouldn't to be taken too seriously, as she said the exact same thing about the Croats during the Bosnian war.

It appears that the latest threat to human health is seal flu. I've been doing what I can to help, going to the end of my nearest pier to shake out sachets of Lemsip. Seals suffer particularly badly from flu, as their flipper length means they can't quite reach their noses with a hankie. I don't think I'd mind so much about seals giving me flu if the little bastards didn't laugh and clap after they'd done it.

Meanwhile, officials have warned that fish pedicures could spread HIV. Why are fish giving pedicures? What is this – *The Flintstones*? *TOWIE* stars have been pictured enjoying the fad, which initially led to worries that the fish could also somehow transmit mental retardation. Of course, the principle of one animal grooming another is quite common in nature. Rhinos have parasites picked from their skin by certain birds, and adult horses are often caught on Facebook posing as foals.

Living in the countryside can apparently increase your risk of getting Parkinson's disease by up to 80 per cent. My grandmother lived on a farm – we knew she had Parkinson's disease when the bulls began queuing to come into the milking shed.

There's talk of a pesticide ban to halt declining bee numbers. I feel partly responsible, as I use their pelts to make pom-poms for my cheerleading hamsters. We must help, as they give us so much. I've been trying to get hold of some beeswax to polish my antique wardrobe but I just can't get the cotton buds in their little ears. Butterfly numbers have also crashed. I say good; for once we can leave our butter out unprotected. I confess I collect the dead ones and dry them out, as my pet mouse just loves flying kites.

Of course, the most common pets in the UK are cats and dogs. It's said that 80 per cent of cat and dog owners display photos of their pet at work. Not me, as I struggle to think straight when I've got an erection. Actually, get this. A survey suggests that 275,000 Swiss people, out of a population of eight million, have sex with animals. No wonder they're so laid back about euthanasia. You're probably laid back about most things once you've pumped a beagle.

A cat sneaked into its owner's suitcase and got into Disney World. The owner was surprised when she opened up her case and found she'd accidentally packed her cat, but not nearly as surprised as her neighbours when they went round to her house to feed her dildo.

A Dutch artist fitted remote-control propellers and turned his dead cat into a toy helicopter. It's not unusual to use beloved pets as toys – I used our tortoise as a goalpost after he died. And immediately before. In many ways it's lovely to see a cat fly without the assistance of an eight-year-old with a banger. It's about time cats caught up – dogs were piloting space rockets way back in the 60s.

Cats that glow in the dark have been created by gene scientists working on a cure for AIDS. But you sense that this is all a prelude to making people with AIDS glow, so when you're in a nightclub you know not to shag them. Scientists have also come up with a fish that glows when exposed to polluted water. Considering the state of the nation's finances,

I fully expect to see all lamp-posts turned off and replaced with plastic bags filled with piss and a luminous mullet doing laps.

Puppies will have to have a chip containing their owners' details in an attempt to stop irresponsible pet ownership. I think that's a great idea. So long as the chip's still readable underwater.

There's been a lot of talk about dangerous dogs. I saw one just this morning playing with one of those things that squeaks when they chew it. What's it called? A toddler. OK, so micro-chipping won't stop them biting. But it might lead to an app to help you get through the park. People do buy dogs without thinking. I got one as I'd heard it was a good way of picking up women. It actually worked, but unfortunately I ended up with a girl who likes having sex with dogs.

Surely the solution is to ban all breeds except poodles. Then you can just get out the clippers and trim it into the shape of your desired breed. If you get hassle from some cretin with a pit bull the trick is to stare into the middle distance while making a low hum. Then slowly move your hand from side to side and this will mesmerise the beast. As for the dog, fuck knows.

A man was left to walk six miles home after he wasn't allowed to take his pet sheep on public transport. He should have worn dark glasses – if anyone had questioned him he could have said it was his guide dog. Then when it was pointed out that it was a sheep he could start crying and say that meant he must have eaten his dog.

SCOTLAND'S JESUS

There's a drug being launched to help depressed dogs. Well, when you keep bringing that stick back just for it to disappear again, you probably start to wonder what the point of life is . . .

9

ECONOMY

The government gives all of your money to the banks so you have to get food from a food bank. No wonder the people of Britain are angry at banks. Sorry, I mean mosques. Bankers are looting the world. You're not in the middle of a recession; you're in the middle of a robbery. It's a robbery and the whole culture is just Stockholm syndrome. When you're actually standing in the City of London it radiates a kind of 1970s sci-fi wrongness. If the country were a person the City would be classified as a disease centre, a wound or a tumour, and al-Qaeda would look suspiciously like chemotherapy.

The reason rich people are so unhappy is that luxury is only designed to be aspired to. It's part of the sales pitch of capitalism – the advert. You're not supposed to actually have it, any more than you're supposed to eat the picture of a hamburger off a menu. Take that holiday brochure in which a waiter serves you a romantic meal on a beach. In reality, your chair leg would sort of sink into the sand at some odd kind of angle and you'd have to shift your weight in the other direction to try to counter it. The table would sink into the sand, too, altering its angle every time you pressed your fork down on to the plate. You would be dimly aware of being annoyed that you could see your waiter smoking under a palm tree between courses. Later, he would startle you by laughing explosively with a passing member of staff and you would vaguely wonder if they were talking about you. There would be little flies everywhere but they wouldn't spoil the food, because all the food would taste of sand.

It's an illness really, the pursuit of wealth. Beyond a certain point money is fucking useless. A pair of diamond-encrusted high-heels costing £276,000 are the most expensive shoes in the world. If you encrust anything with enough diamonds it can be the world's most expensive. Stick a £50 note in dog shit and you've got a world record.

Only the very rich and the very poor can boast about the sheer act of having bought a thing. For the middle classes it's all about connoisseurship. You can't boast about your spending power, so instead it's about your taste, as you burrow deeper and deeper into the marketed life. Connoisseurship is what used to be boasted of by merchants – 'Look at all the lovely stuff I've gathered to sell.' We're still merchants but now we're selling the idea of ourselves. And, of course, our personal taste is largely meaningless, but it's all we've got, so we give it the force of moral judgement.

I'm studying for the economics of the future, trying to find out as much as possible about the currency potential of gold teeth, homemade antibiotics and monkey slaves. Soon, the days when our lives were dominated by the confidence people felt in the relative values of fictions that we watched through electronic screens will seem to our embattled children like we worshiped river spirits and forest dryads.

We could be in the worst financial crisis since the 1930s. That's judging by the three main measures: GDP, employment and the size of coin most people would be prepared to pick out of a urinal. And to this day my gran still uses Bisto instead of stockings. Can't say I approve; seems to me to be a pretty racist way of robbing a post office. But don't despair, there are lots of ways to make a bit of extra cash. My tip is to go along to your local shopping centre dressed as a fountain.

Quantitative easing and low interest rates are just ways to make money for speculators by taking it almost directly from savers. There's no point in saving any more. I've less interest in my bank account than I have in the Blue reunion. William Hague's said there's only one true growth strategy for the UK. Work harder. Advice that really paid off for that horse in *Animal Farm*. But he's right. Unless we can at least look industrious, in a few years' time the Chinese might overlook us and buy Spain or Ireland instead.

New disability proposals will affect me directly as I'm the owner of a prosthetic rubber fist that has resulted in my girlfriend being on disability benefits. Can she still claim? Iain Duncan Smith said he could live on £53 a week and a petition is challenging him to give it a go. Of course Iain could live on £53 a week. He makes more than that a day trawling ponds in children's hospitals for loose change. He calls it 'fishing for dreams'.

There was a petition to try to make him give it a go. That just focuses things on personalities. Campaigns focusing on the victims of policy now seem unthinkable. The real purpose of housing-benefit changes is to force the poor out of city centres so they can be defended during the 2018 *X Factor* sex riots. Water cannon used to disperse the sex riots will destroy a branch of Lush, turning the protest into a seething, anarchist Manumission. All the beefs of the UK grime scene will be forgotten as I pilot a hover-platform of top MCs over the sex riots, frothing it to our pulsing beats.

Surely far better than him living on £53 would be for Iain to live with a family on a council estate while living the exact same lifestyle that he does at present. Would it not be a more chilling reminder of class difference if he's sitting in front of the TV, while two kids eat fish fingers complaining that they can't see their cartoons because they're being blocked by Iain's cheese trolley?

Let's not forget that being a minister is a precarious existence. If Iain loses his job at the next election he'll be just like the rest of us, forced to accept some directorship for a meagre six-figure salary, in exchange for spending two days a week helping them add the maximum mark-up when flogging stuff to the next government. Will any coalition ministers take up the challenge of trying to live on benefits? Well, after 2015 I suspect plenty of Lib Dems will.

Of course, George Osborne is right and the only way to teach those bankers a lesson is to cut benefits. Just as the only way to fix the NHS is to leave a jar of beetroot outside the Stafford branch of WH Smith. The government says the shake-up in the benefits system is to make people less dependent on state handouts (and presumably a lot more dependent on drugs and alcohol). It wouldn't surprise me if the Tories' next big scheme was to create a network of tunnels that connected all the wishing wells across the country together, so all the pennies thrown in to grant children's wishes could be collected in a central government vault that was then used to purchase MPs' bed linen.

I can't believe that woman who was swindling £42,000 a year in benefits by claiming to have imaginary kids. It's immoral. Call me old-fashioned but that line should only be used to make it easier to offload new partners you've lost interest in. Seriously, if you know someone cheating the benefit system you really must act without delay. A simple bit of blackmail and you could be getting half their claim.

George Osborne exploited the anger and grief over the deaths of six children to further his case for welfare cuts. Bear in mind that if the welfare state were adequately funded social services might have had a chance to save these children. Mick Philpott and the Chancellor have more in common than you might imagine. They both live in houses with a snooker room paid for by taxpayers; both are hated by the public and if they were left unguarded on B Wing they'd both be stripped to the bone like an aromatic crispy duck at a late-night casino buffet.

George Osborne has vowed to guide Britain through the looming threat of a double-dip recession. Straight into a triple-dip recession. Of course, a recession means more charities hassling us in the streets. I'd never make out a standing order for starving Africans. Donate the same amount on the same day each month and they'll just get complacent. Far better to make sporadic visits and dance through their dusty village with a silver-topped cane throwing out coins and sherbet fountains. Or turn up on a random day being wheeled through their huts on a cart so they can suckle nutritional syrup from my giant, translucent prosthetic abdomen with cries of 'Señor Abeja! Señor Abeja está aquí!' ('Mr Bee! Mr Bee is here!').

I should add, there's not a single Third World village where people enjoy students turning up for a gap year. Just send them your airfare, you fucking grief tourists.

The Chancellor has predicted six more years of pain. It'll be more painful for some than others. Especially George Osborne. He won't ever get an injection from a nurse that doesn't hit a nerve. He'll never again be able to pass through border control without getting a thorough cavity search. For the rest of his life even something as simple as wandering around a museum is going to be filled with misery, when he returns to the cloak-room to find someone has shat in his coat pocket. Why's George so insistent that he stick to plan A? It's like a bomb-disposal expert deciding on day one of his career that he's only ever going to cut the black wire. I'm not going to question the expertise of a man who was a millionaire by the age of thirty (his age, coincidentally, when his trust fund paid out).

He's promised us free childcare and faster broadband – an ideal combination. If you're at home in a tear-stained nest of job-rejection letters the last thing you need is a toddler walking in on you during a mood-boosting wank. Motorists won a victory when it was announced that the 3p rise in fuel duty has been scrapped. So no doubt people all over the country will be delighted that it's now going to be slightly less expensive than they first thought to gas themselves this Christmas.

I love the Budget. It's great that we've set aside a time of year when a multi-millionaire tells us how much we should pay for fags and a pint. Everyone is agreed that Osborne's Budget was far worse than we could have hoped for. I was hoping he was going to have an uncontrollable nose bleed that led to his death, slipping around on the floor of the House desperately trying to regain his footing like a dying cow, so I've got to say it was hugely disappointing. To be fair, the government has created loads more small businesses. Mainly by shrinking large ones.

All around Britain families always have no idea if the Budget has made them better or worse off, but there's a simple way of working it out – it's worse. Last year Osborne got rid of the 50p tax rate for top earners, meaning they're now only dodging a 45p tax rate. I'm not sure the poor would mind paying extra taxes. The trick would be to have Osborne and Cameron crank out a few Adele numbers, then nick it off them in a text vote.

Osborne has employed what have been described as 'stealth' taxes on the elderly. Why the stealth? Remember these are old people; they have their televisions on so loud you could creep up on them in a Formula 1 car.

A report has warned of a crisis in funding for our rapidly ageing population. The government says it's patronising to think that pensioners aren't capable of still contributing to the economy. So, in a decade expect to see your grandparents tottering knock-kneed to and from the airport giving piggybacks to Chinese businessmen. More people will have to move back in with their kids. It worked for my granddad. Dad loved taking him out for drives in the country. Right up till he heard shouting through the cat flap and knew he'd found his way home again. When I pass seventy I'm planning to have myself surgically Siamese-twinned with my lad – I thought my arse to his shoulder, then he can pass me off as a guardian angel. I'm looking forward to a contented old age of shitting down his back like a pirate's parrot.

We now have automatic workplace pensions. Ignore those who say £2 a week won't lead to a good payout from the Post Office. Come retirement it should provide just enough for some tights and a shotgun. Extra pensions could have been done through National Insurance, but the Tories thought the safest thing was to utilise the evident skills of the financial sector. Is it such a bad thing we have to work in old age? If Nana's rounding up trolleys at ASDA it could be a great way to get the weekly shop and the grandparent visit done in one go. Besides, the increasing shortage of NHS dentists means plenty of us will have removable falsies, a real asset if to make ends meet you have to go on the game.

People always say that no matter what the Chancellor does he'll never make everybody happy. I beg to differ, as throwing himself from the viewing deck of the Shard would be guaranteed to raise public morale. Osborne joined Twitter and got abused – what did he expect? Someone who innocently got retweeted by Justin Bieber received death threats, let alone a prick who actually deserves it. This year the economy will grow by 0.6 per cent. To put that into perspective, we could make the economy grow by 5 per cent if everyone who reads this book went straight out afterwards and bought a bag of crisps. I haven't seen figures this grim since I judged the Miss Dundee pageant.

Royal Bank of Scotland boss Stephen Hester handed back his £1 million bonus. Iain Duncan Smith said Hester should give up his bonus but that the government couldn't make him do so. That's right, the government is totally powerless to tell people what to do – hence the fact we're all allowed to smoke marijuana and keep chimps as pets. Hester says he gave it back because he didn't want to become a pariah – that's good, I was worried he'd done it because it was the right thing to do.

Barclays were fined for 'manipulating the Libor'. I'm so disgusted with them I plan to take my custom elsewhere. From now on I'll be nicking my pens from Argos. The fine of £240 million has taught Barclays a valuable lesson. That fixing rates is worth it. Why is Bob Diamond always referred to as 'one of Britain's top bankers'? He lost Barclays £290 million. My son still has the fiver his granny gave him for Christmas, which makes him a more successful banker than Bob Diamond. Fuck it, on the figures alone my couch is a better banker than Bob Diamond.

Hundreds of bankers might be prosecuted for fraud, following the rate-rigging scandal. They'd better have good lawyers or they could end up in jail. Unfortunately, they do and they won't. Allowing MPs to investigate the banks is like getting Premier League football teams to investigate the sex industry.

Disgraced former HBOS banker Sir James Crosby asked for his own knighthood to be removed. Of course, it's better to hand it back yourself rather than sit and wait for the Queen to come and take it off you by force. This is terrible news for Crosby – without his knighthood he won't be allowed free access to museums, exhibitions and English Heritage buildings. I don't think giving the knighthood back is enough – I think he should have his shoulders cut off so he can never receive one again. Perhaps it's even time for an award that's the opposite of a knighthood. Just so we can fully show our gratitude to bankers and the like, the Queen could tap their shoulders with a dirty mop and blow a raspberry, before they wriggle out the room on their stomachs while Prince Philip flicks them with a wet towel.

Boris Johnson's warned the government that new bank regulations could risk 'killing the goose'. I'm guessing that's from the expression 'Don't kill the goose that lays the golden eggs made from all that money we've all already fed the goose anyway.' The deadline for the banks to make the changes is 2019, giving us the structure that's needed to avoid a second banking crisis, just after a second banking crisis has already taken place. I'm not worried about the banking problems as I keep all my money in Jersey. Not in a bank but buried in the garden of a children's care home. They won't look there.

The recession has led to an increase in lending and there are new laws to clamp down on loan sharks. The industry still insists they receive few complaints, then again it can be hard to type an email in a plaster cast, especially when your laptop's in Cash Converters . . . and it's surprising how important teeth turn out to be in forming coherent speech.

Payday loan firms have been told to sort out their dodgy practices. Some have hit back, pointing out that without them as a safety net many people could fall dangerously behind on their online bingo commitments. The move was prompted by news of an imminent cash loans advertising push, started by rumours that Carol Vorderman was to have her eyes surgically replaced with slowly rotating spiral discs. The loans are supposed to be just till the next payday. But the way the economy's going for a lot of people that's not expected to be till 2018.

• • •

A study claims people in the most deprived parts of the country are spending a fortune on fruit machines. The government is genuinely concerned, as all the cash it's diverting from the lottery could bring an end to subsidised opera. I used to have a gambling problem with the horses. I'd always want to play poker, but they'd insist on snap.

The government should at least bring back the one-armed bandits. Otherwise in a decade's time the urban poor won't even have the strength and dexterity to open their door for the monthly visit of the man who liposucks out their fat reserves to be rendered down for biodiesel.

The cost of lottery tickets is to double. Or put another way, the UK has announced a 100 per cent increase in tax on the poor. A risky move by lottery bosses Camelot, it could threaten Tory hopes to appoint them to run the NHS. The prize for five numbers will be halved, meaning people will soon have virtually no chance of winning £50,000 rather than virtually no chance of winning £100,000. It's part of a bigger rebranding of the lottery, including changing the logo to just a single raised middle finger.

We all have our ways of picking the numbers. I tend to write numbers on forty-four eggs then place them in a giant incubator. When they've hatched and matured, I ride the biggest ostrich at the head of all the rest, tether it up outside the newsagents and ask for a Lucky Dip. Though of late I've swallowed forty-four numbered ping pong balls, then jotted down the first six that I reflexively regurgitate when played the *Loose Women* theme tune.

A high proportion of lottery players are older women. So an easy way to guarantee some pretty vigorous action with over-fifties divorcees is just to get your cock coated in scratch-card foil. I think if I won it'd be important to share that kind of wealth. I'd have a hundred grand changed into 2p coins, put in a tip-up truck, then I'd drive round looking for buskers. I'd also get a penis extension. Nothing too big, just a room big enough to display them all in.

Some of the sums being won are ridiculous. What would I do with that kind of money? It's a cliché but I'd have one fore-arm replaced with an outboard motor. Then I could commit a crime near any body of water and skilfully avoid detection by tipping Fairy Liquid from my hollow top hat and thrashing the surface with the propeller, before disappearing into the spume.

Ray Winstone says he'll leave this country as he's being 'raped' by high taxes. I hope he moves to a country where they have no taxes. And he's then raped. Most people would happily pay more tax if they thought it was going towards raping Ray Winstone. That could be the new television advert for HMRC come self-assessment time: the little tax collector cartoon character in a pinstripe suit and bowler hat raping Ray Winstone. I reckon you'd get people earning seven grand a year offering to pay 40 per cent tax.

Stamps are to rise by a staggering 30 per cent. Maybe the Post Office should try to appease public anger by at least having the Queen lower her top to expose a nipple. If you've little kids you can save money; they'll think it's a real adventure delivering the easier ones for you. Which reminds me, I must phone the Congolese embassy again. I know, I'll never forgive myself; if I hadn't treated him to all those extra crusts he'd have been able to squeeze out through the bars like normal.

Research shows there's a 'fine line between being willing to pay more and walking away from the service' – a line that was crossed about eight years ago. In their defence, the Royal Mail have had to raise prices because there's less birthday money in cards for their postmen to steal nowadays. The postal service is to be sold off, with staff receiving £2,000 in shares. Not all employees will receive them, as they'll be sent out by post. The government has been warned there could be striking at the Royal Mail, but sadly for the unions people thought they already were.

Ed Miliband called for all UK goods to display 'Made in Britain' stickers. Aren't our exports suffering enough as it is?

We might shift a bit more with ones that say 'Made in Germany' (or Japan). It's a good idea for electrical stuff. Then I could cancel my *Which?* subscription as I wouldn't need them to tell me the worst buys. Surely we're in enough trouble with the likes of al-Qaeda as it is without their operatives glancing at a tiny Union flag on the clamps being fastened to their testicles by the Saudi police?

It seems there are now four hundred and ten different UK gas tariffs. The cheapest way to keep warm must be to get hold of all the different companies' promotional literature. Burning it should see you through till spring. David Cameron has promised to reduce gas and electricity bills. He's planning to do this by making as many people as possible homeless. No, he actually made energy companies send a letter to their customers. He denies that's all he's done to help people heat their houses, pointing out that they can always put the letter on a saucer and burn it. It's a particularly helpful development for all those many internet-savvy eighty-year-olds who like to research what the cost of freezing to death this winter will be. An advisory letter? If I'm going to stay I at least want some petrol-station flowers and a huge card with an embossed puppy on it.

Dave says insulation is essential. That's true. If there's any hint of heat escaping from your house local pensioners will surround it like in *Dawn of the Dead*. Do keep an eye on your local elderly during the cold weather. Remember, all it takes to sneak into some people's wills is a couple of trips to the Co-op.

The Energy Saving Trust has found out that overfilling our kettles wastes £68 million per year. Which is nothing compared with the amount of energy wasted by the Energy Saving Trust coming up with that fucking useless statistic. If the Trust really wanted to save some energy the first thing they should do is sack the team of scientists who were boiling kettles 9 to 5, seven days a week for a year, turn off the website and board up the office. They recommend that by cutting just one minute from our showering time we'd save £215 million a year. Life's tough enough. Which would you rather: spending an extra minute in the shower every day getting away from your problems or once every three months not even noticing that you'd saved forty pence? Here's an easy way to cut energy usage – imprint 'Do you really need to?' on all light switches in braille.

Ofgem criticised the big six gas and electricity firms for their lack of transparency. Which is odd, because they can't be more transparently a bunch of money-grabbing bastards. Research shows 70 per cent of people pay too much to their energy supplier because they're on the wrong tariff. The other 30 per cent pay too much to their energy supplier because they're on the right tariff.

How nice of them to freeze prices this winter. It explains why they were continually putting them up over the summer. So we have to continually search for a better deal. Basically, the energy firms are like an abusive spouse: the more loyal we are, the more we get punished. Ministers have vowed to fine energy firms that fiddle gas and electricity prices. However, will they think of a way of paying such fines?

Energy prices are rising at such a rate that many people will have to go back to the traditional method of heating their home on a cold winter's night. Getting pissed and setting fire to it with the chip pan.

The elderly are, of course, particularly vulnerable, as nobody gives a fuck about them. Scottish Gas has put heating prices out of reach for so many pensioners they're thinking of rebranding themselves as 'DigniGas'. The government won't act, as the projected springtime surge in the number of estate agents after the hypothermia cull is its only current plan to cut unemployment figures.

David Cameron says he wants to restart the Right to Buy scheme so council tenants can share the same dreams as home-owners. I wonder if he means the one where you're eating shredded newspaper so you can pay the mortgage or the one where you're trapped in a loveless marriage by negative equity. The UK has the smallest new homes in Europe. Many new homes are only as big as a London tube carriage. A good comparison. In my experience both often contain at least one woman who can't bring herself to make eye contact.

House prices are continuing to drop. Experts fear that if the trend continues property might soon only be worth something close to its actual value. A house in Wales is on sale for zero pounds. It's so dilapidated you'd have to be mad to live there. And yet three million people do. The poor have nothing to fear from the recession. It's just about being resourceful. Simply pop into a branch of Millets just before 6pm and when the assistant's not looking sneak into one of the display tents.

High-street sales fell over Christmas for the first time in four years as millions of shoppers switched to the internet. After all, why go out shopping in the cold and rain, and be jostled by crowds of strangers, when you can stay at home and watch porn? Let's face it, Tesco would go bust if someone could email us a sandwich. People now do preliminary research in the real world but inevitably finish up online – a vision of the decline of the UK high street . . . and of the sex life of most men over thirty.

The big high-street chains are really suffering, which is a shame considering the amount of effort they've made over the last twenty-five years to force local shops out of business. It's a real pity that so many HMVs have gone. Now where will I go when I want to ignore a World Music section? HMV is ninety-two years old, which probably explains why it doesn't know anything about downloading music or films from the internet. I actually preferred going into HMV than buying things from Amazon – mainly because when I was in a shop I was much less likely to get distracted and have a wank instead.

And poor Jessops. Such a cruel irony that the high street's leading seller of telescopes failed to see it coming. It's unfortunate, but maybe they should have considered opening branches of their camera shop somewhere that people would use them – like the 80s.

Blockbuster went block bust. This was a real shock, as most people thought it had closed down years ago. A Blockbuster spokesman said, 'The core business is still profitable.' What, films? Yes, they are. But renting out an old DVD copy of *Dances with Wolves* for two days? Not so much. It's certainly a shock to me. Who would have thought clicking a mouse could ever replace trudging through the sleet to be told you need three not two forms of ID?

And Little Chef is up for sale. You know you're in trouble when even truckers turn their noses up at your food. Who could forget that illuminated sign? Even now I reflexively salivate if my headlamps swing across a fat man while I'm parking at a dogging site. We used to get taken there on birthdays. This might have been more of a treat if Dad had had a car. They are pricey, though. I prefer to gaffer-tape a shrimp net on to a three-metre pole and stick it vertically through the sun roof. Before long you're stuffing your face with engine-warmed starling.

Tesco scrapped plans for hypermarkets and will instead open another 830 smaller convenience stores. They realised that after they'd killed off the high street with out-of-town shopping centres there was now plenty of town-centre retail space going cheap. They're opening up so many smaller shops that eventually they will all link up with each other, forming one huge, long, snakelike convenience store that will then dislocate its jaw and eat Britain.

There was a storm when a graduate, Cait Reilly, was backed by the courts for saying stacking shelves violated her human rights. She said stacking shelves in Poundland was 'slave labour'. I don't remember the bit in *Amistad* when Cinqué was flogged for not replenishing the Simply Fruity Apple and Blackcurrant four-packs. Cait has a degree in geology so it's surprising she can't find work – I thought the ability to recognise a rock would be recession-proof. Judging by the staff in my local branch she might have more luck getting the RSPCA involved. To be honest, I'm more a fan of the 99p Stores. It gives me the chance to play the big shot at the tills with a cheeky wink and a 'keep the change'.

Still, I completely agreed with her. How cruel is it to make someone work in a shop with the name Poundland and then not give them any pounds? It's worse than sending a homeless person with no shoes to work in Boots. It's worse than sending a victim of floods to work in Monsoon. It's worse than sending a dyslexic man called Austin to work in Austin Reed.

Europe's largest shopping centre opened its doors in East London. In ten years' time it will have a Cash for Gold supermarket and in twenty years it will be Europe's largest zombie-containment centre. Leading economist Douglas McWilliams has suggested the economy could be boosted just by axing all bank holidays. Why stop there? Can you imagine how much the economy would benefit from having us strapped to desks and lathes as Mr McWilliams milks us or extracts our viable eggs with a Dyson crevice tool to mix in a huge breeding pond to create the next generation of wage slaves?

Maybe the Occupy movement was the last glimmer of hope, a chance to generate a few stories to tell in the sex camps. Two hundred and fifty people took part in the Occupy London protest. Sadly, they'd have needed a few more bodies before they could have occupied London. With those sort of numbers they could barely occupy screen six at Cineworld. Protestors said we've internalised the attitudes of capitalism – I thought, 'I'll buy that.' It was amazing to read the protestors' demands – common-sense measures like equality, less money to bankers, more to health services. Soon, we'll have to camp out for three months just to ask not to be shot in the face. I find it incredible that people should have to protest against giving the bankers – who fucked us – money. It's like asking prostitutes to pay their clients, and as I know from bitter experience that almost never works.

10

CELEBS

I wonder if the whole celebrity world isn't just a group of people displacing their need for parental attention. They're remarkably like children: the tears; the sibling-like rivalries; their bodies changing in front of us. That makes us the parents, and really bad ones at that: living vicariously through them; judging their life choices; fancying some of them.

There are nearly seven billion people on planet earth. Which makes it all the more baffling that we know Danny Dyer's name. If anyone deserves to be famous shouldn't it be the woman who walks a fifteen-mile round trip to collect fresh drinking water for her family? I'd love for her to become a celebrity. Her dieting video would be a no-brainer. It would be great to see her in the green room on *The Jonathan Ross Show*, bantering with Louie Spence and David Walliams, exchanging anecdotes about deadly diseases they've had and what it's like to be raped. Eventually, fame would change her and we'd see her falling out of China White, balancing a jero-boam of vintage Perrier-Jouët champagne on her head. Although the papers will of course 'conveniently' fail to report that although she was in Soho, she'd kept it real and walked from Plymouth.

Researchers have found that being famous shortens your lifespan. I suppose that's the only consolation we have when Piers Morgan's TV show gets another series. Katy Perry is sick of fame. At least, that's what she tweeted to her 4.3 million followers. She says fame is a 'disgusting by-product' of what she does. I thought the disgusting by-product of what she does was her music.

TOWIE's Kirk Norcross says fame left him feeling depressed and suffering from paranoia and panic attacks. Another way of phrasing that might be depression left him fantasising that he was famous.

For the genuinely famous, it's true there are dangers. Hugh Jackman was attacked by a stalker, who was arrested for throwing an electric razor filled with her pubic hair at him while screaming, 'I love you!' Well, if she did love him she's got a funny way of showing it. No, genuinely. It was a very funny way of showing it.

The Joss Stone samurai-sword trial was certainly a security wake-up call for me. From now on I'm only dressing up as a white female soul singer in my mid-twenties with the curtains drawn. The men accused of plotting to kill her also wanted to kill Craig David, R. Kelly and Chris Brown. To be fair, they've got a point. It's absolutely crazy that these men wanted to kill Joss Stone because of her connections with the royal family and not because of her music. I suspect they'll try and win the sympathy of the jury by claiming they planned to use that sword to cut off her tongue. The judge decided to jail them, despite calls from the public gallery to release them after giving them One Direction's home addresses.

A divorced dad of two threatened to kidnap Tamara Ecclestone unless he was paid £900,000. He'd have been more likely to have got the money if he'd threatened to not kidnap her. There's no point in kidnappers taking Tamara hostage as they'd never be able to meet her demands.

She also received anonymous threats from someone who said they'd reveal details about her personal life. She's horrified that someone could do that to her without paying her for them. I just hope she's been getting my threats about what I'll do if she doesn't stop revealing details of her private life.

She was photographed lying naked, spread-eagled on a million pounds in cash. I saw something very similar this weekend in Glasgow. Although, in fairness, the guy wasn't totally naked. His pants and trousers were around his ankles, and the cash he was sprawled across added up to less than three quid in change. And the photographer wasn't from a tabloid but worked for the coroner's office.

Tamara is getting a £1 million crystal bath. Her life would make a good docusoap. She lights some scented candles, runs a lemongrass and jasmine bubble bath, and puts on some relaxing whale music. But who's this at the door? Why, it's Ian Huntley with his dog Sadie. Let's leave everybody together for fifteen minutes and see what they get up to.

Taylor Swift received death threats on Twitter after it was revealed she was dating Harry Styles. Hearing that young girls are so obsessed with Harry they want to murder whoever dates him makes me so sad. So sad he isn't dating Jessie J. I heard Taylor couldn't match Harry's previous partners in the bedroom, as she often tucked him in way too tight.

Harry was also linked with the considerably older Caroline Flack. Apparently, he's really good in bed – he can get straight off to sleep without needing a story. There can be many benefits to dating a woman twice your age. Never underestimate the benefits of removable teeth. Terrific for edging pastry.

The papers described Harry as 'Randy Styles'. He's eighteen. You show me a non-randy eighteen-year-old boy and I will show you someone lying to their girlfriend's dad.

One Direction remind me of hospital superbugs. You know there's quite a few, but no one can name more than two of them. Like any great boy band you can tell who is which by their personality traits: the quiet one, the quiet one, the quiet one, the quiet one and the gerontophile. They made history as the first UK pop group to début at number one on the US Billboard album chart. So if you have that on 'This is a dead planet' bingo, cross it out and then shout 'House!' as you lay your head on the line and the freight train barrels towards you.

One Direction played Madison Square Garden (a venue that's hosted Led Zeppelin, The Who and The Rolling Stones). It's surely the musical equivalent of racing pigs in a synagogue. Their luck, fame and lack of talent don't upset me, provided I can convince myself I'm actually just lying in a darkened room somewhere experiencing a *Total Recall*-style implant installed by my nemesis.

One Direction's predecessors JLS split up. I immediately set up a helpline – it gives out suggestions of how we can get rid of other shit bands. JLS explained they wanted to go out on a high. But I guess they just got fed up waiting, so decided to split anyway. They've said they'll only be seen together now for charity events. In which case I'm sure I can rustle up fifty quid for them to appear on *Comic Relief* as a human centipede.

JLS broke the mould for boy bands with a radical, fresh approach that saw just three of them wear hats. Marvin said, 'We don't want to be that band that people get fed up of.' It's a pity they didn't feel that way five years ago. People mocked them and said they would never achieve anything in music but they went on to prove all the doubters correct. Britain's music industry won't be the same without them. It'll be slightly better.

Let's not forget that in 2010 their music brought a teenager out of a coma. Though sadly she couldn't reach the CD player off-switch so went for the one on her life support instead. JLS say they're going to work on solo projects. Why don't boy bands ever come up with something more interesting to do after they split? For once, at the press conference I'd like one of them to announce that he's going to spend a lot more of his time doing ad hoc medical experiments on himself, before slipping his T-shirt off to reveal his back is covered in ears.

Talking about a medical experiment, Jordan spoke at the University of Oxford, summarising her life and career in less than eight minutes. Which may sound short, but actually it's rather impressive as I know I could summarise her life and career in one word. But it would be a word so filled with sorrow and pain it would be like the noise a mermaid makes when it's been harpooned through the heart by a Japanese whaler. She joked that she 'wouldn't want to play Trivial Pursuit with any of you'. I'd love to see it happen. It'd be like watching the supercomputer Big Blue play chess against a fridge freezer.

I'm not sure if you caught Jordan's last show, *Signed by Katie Price*. It's already been sold abroad and Al-Qaeda want it as their next promotional video. The show was her biggest on-screen flop since the stitching on her left tit gave way while she was recording an exercise video. The episode I saw was a cross between a *Robocop* insert and the images that would flood your mind if a vampire bit you in the forehead.

Katie Price got married again, this time to a male stripper. He's also a builder, which will be handy in a couple of years when her tits need scaffolding. New hubby Kieran looked delighted, his only moment of doubt coming when Katie caught her own bouquet. At least she's finally found a partner who can stand up to her. If there's one sort of man that won't let a woman tell them what to do it's a stripper. She even chose the wedding cake that he jumped out of. She wants to give her kids a bit of stability by having a new father for the next six months.

I know he wanted to make an honest woman of her but considering the amount of rubber, silicon and plastic in her body a more honest woman could be created by drawing a smiley face on to a filing cabinet. They say he didn't stay down on one knee for long, as he was unnerved by the voice emanating from her knickers, growling 'feed me souls' like a haunted mirror in a Hammer film. Hopefully, their combined IQ might be just large enough to outsmart the yeast infection in danger of taking control of her cerebral cortex.

The ceremony took place in the Bahamas, Katie's favourite holiday destination; she often pops over for a week or two to let her tan fade. There were only six guests this time, presumably as it'll be less hassle sending the presents back. Katie said the decision to marry Kieran was a no-brainer. I think I'd already worked that one out for myself.

She wanted the wedding to be classy, which wasn't easy when she'd invited herself. She could have hired the Ritz for her reception but as soon as she stepped in it would have felt like a Chicken Cottage.

Katie says staff at the resort where she married asked her if she was a porn star. Nope. Just a keen amateur. Honestly, the vulgar assumptions people make just because you've been fitted with a giant pair of plastic tits. She slammed the atmosphere at the Sandals resort as being like a Club 18-30 holiday. To be fair, it couldn't have been. Or she'd have been asked to leave when they saw the date of birth on her passport. She also complained that their sun-loungers were plastic. I can see how that would have been upsetting – for her new husband to look at her and not know where the lounger stopped and she began. Every time Katie has sex she must think men can't get enough of her body as they run their hands all over her. What she fails to understand is that it's just a reflex action and they're simply looking for the nozzle to deflate her.

Katie Price wannabe Jodie Marsh is still appearing everywhere. I'm not sure what she's promoting, but from the look of her it's homosexuality. She looks like a hilarious mix-up in a toy factory in which Barbie's head has been chewed by a dog before being accidentally placed on Action Man's body. It looks like in less than two months she has gone from a size ten, to a complete mental breakdown. She's been spending five hours a day working out in the gym and three hours a day standing in a garden being creosoted.

Jodie Marsh launched a slimming pill called Semtex, causing outrage among families of IRA victims. Her shameless lack of tact has really blown up in her face this time. The pill helps you lose weight by making you get down on your knees every five minutes to check under your car.

Jodie was voted the 32nd best bum in the United Kingdom. Which sounds disappointing until you realise that her tits came 145,877 and her face didn't even meet the entry standard. Jodie says she loves her body and would run naked through a crowded street if you asked her to. I'm asking. But I'm adding one stipulation: the street must be in Tehran.

What is it with these celebrities' obsession with plastic surgery? There's something at once very morbid and childlike in knowing that Death is coming, but thinking that he won't recognise you in your little plastic mask.

Amy Childs has had her second boob job to enhance her breasts from a 32C to a 32DD. Getting a tit wank from Amy Childs must be like sticking your knob between the tyres of a stationary HGV. Meanwhile, Gwyneth Paltrow has been having injections of bee venom and reckons she no longer notices the pain of an old injury . . . thanks to the pain of hundreds of bee stings.

Her pal Madonna's carcass looks like something you'd boil up to make soup. I'll bet her bathwater tastes delicious. She appears to have had some dodgy Botox. They've had to update her waxwork in Madame Tussauds by giving it a right-hook, left-cross combination. I'm not saying Madge has lost her looks but I confess some sperm I ejaculated watching the video for 'Like a Virgin' in the 80s has just found its way back under my front door and crawled back down my urethra.

Victoria Beckham's been having sheep-placenta gel massaged into her face. If £500 million in the bank isn't enough to enable her to crack a smile I doubt smearing afterbirth on her face is going to. Easy to mock, but I've done similar myself. A last-minute fancy-dress invite found me with only lamb chops in the fridge, so I had to go as Noddy Holder.

Beyoncé had a baby by elective caesarean, of course. Many celebrities are so desperate to avoid a visible scar that surgeons now make the incision beneath the armpit, then massage the baby round . . . I'm told it's a bit like trying to get a cat out of a duvet cover. Beyoncé cleverly kept a low profile by checking in under the name Ingrid Jackson. So when anyone asked, 'Who's just paid $1 million to rent the entire floor of the hospital?' the answer was, 'Oh, just that plain old Ingrid Jackson that Jay-Z keeps visiting.'

You don't need to spend that much to get a bit of space in a maternity ward. Do what I did, and check your partner in as Maxine Carr. Beyoncé said of motherhood, 'I actually feel like my child introduced me to myself.' Luckily for her she's a multi-millionaire celebrity. If she were a single mum living in a council flat she could have her kid taken off her for less than that.

Beyoncé and Jay-Z are spending $1 million a year renting out a nursery for their daughter at a basketball stadium. When I was a kid my parents spent some money on a nursery for me to sit in while they were busy. We called it 'the car'.

Beyoncé is going to be the new face of Pepsi. And by face, they mean arse. Someone needs to remind Pepsi that they can pay £30 million for a superstar to advertise their product but the advert might as well say, 'What? They don't have Coke? OK then, if there's no Lilt then I suppose I'll have a Pepsi.'

• • •

Michael Jackson's family are accusing concert promoters AEG of only caring about money, by launching a $40 billion lawsuit against them. They're saying the promoters forced Jacko to perform, which then led to his death. Unlike Jacko's family, as when they forced him to perform it only led to an emotionally stunted, self-loathing, body-dysmorphic, drugged, addicted man-child who sought escapism in the company of children and monkeys. They say that the jury will see some ugly stuff – they're not kidding. The rest of the Jacksons look like Halloween on the burns unit. Katherine Jackson says she didn't want AEG to force Jacko into performing when it could have damaged his health – she'd have rather they'd used one of the more disposable members of the family, like Jermaine.

AEG claim that Jacko was keeping his health problems a secret. A secret? Well, hardly – he looked like something you'd pass on a ghost train. If AEG lose the case they'll have to pay out $40 billion – what can they put on to raise that sort of cash? I'm guessing they're trying to work out if some jump leads will reanimate Jacko's corpse. Courtroom details are sketchy but there were claims AEG responded to rumours of Jacko's fits and rampant pill-popping by cynically suggesting more maraca solos. Jacko was given very strong drugs to help him sleep – to be fair, if every time I closed my eyes I could see Macaulay Culkin doing that screaming face I'd need an anaesthetic as well.

His children say Jacko did everything he could to give them a normal childhood – and speaking as someone who grew up on a merry-go-round with a baboon as a wet nurse I think he did a great job of it. It'll be interesting to see if the kids display any of Jacko's personality traits – you know, his little foibles like living on a rollercoaster and being best friends with a circus.

Former *Oliver!* star Mark Lester claimed he's the father of Jacko's daughter Paris. If Mark is the father it could be a chance for the kids to lead a more normal life – and it's coming to something when moving in with a grown-up Oliver Twist on the other side of the world is 'more normal'. This sort of attention isn't good for kids – or anybody – and it was no surprise to see our easily outraged tabloids using a kid's suicide in an attempt to sell copies.

Meanwhile, Justin Bieber's increasingly bizarre behaviour has worried some that he might be turning into the new

Jacko. He's even building a zoo. Hopefully, he won't use the zoo to indulge his sick urges. Apparently, Jacko would often coat his buttocks in sand, before inverting himself and getting his butler to startle the ostriches. Still, the man's dead. We should remember him in happier times: dangling a baby out of a window perhaps, or sharing a bed with three nine-year-olds while a bemused Liz Taylor scraped up llama turds with a gold disc.

Bieber failed to collect his pet monkey from quarantine so he's gone to a zoo. It's the best place for him. Whereas the best place for the monkey would be back in the jungle. I hope that ten years from now a giant silverback gorilla turns up at Bieber's door and says, 'Why did you leave me, Daddy?' before ripping his face off. And for anyone who's thinking 'Monkeys don't grow into gorillas', may I just point out they can't work doorbells, either.

Justin Bieber left a message in the visitors' book at Anne Frank's house hoping that if Anne were alive she would be a fan of his. If Anne Frank were alive she'd be eighty-four years old. She'd much more likely be targeted by Harry from One Direction.

Bieber was caught on camera spitting off a balcony as a crowd of fans gathered below. It's not the first time he's treated his fans with utter disdain, as there's also his music. He's a multi-millionaire who turned nineteen earlier this year – of course he acts badly. It's not going to be a tremendous shock when he turns into a transsexual antiques expert.

● ● ●

I agree with Michael Douglas. The only way to promote your biopic of a gay icon is to say 'I ate so much pussy I got cancer.' Turns out Douglas only smoked to get the taste of pussy out of his mouth. I'm worried that these revelations mean they're going to ban cunnilingus in pubs. Thing is, if we found out that all cancer was caused by oral sex we'd still have to find a cure for cancer.

We mustn't overreact. I'd suggest compulsory testing, and anyone who comes up positive just gets their pubes shaved into a skull and crossbones. Michael does less of that sort of thing now as he often finds himself coming up again unsure what he went down for in the first place. His cunnilingus habit was actually a side effect of his excessive sex drive – his penis had become so exhausted that at the mere hint of an available woman it would bury its head in his scrotum in the manner of a sleeping swan.

Michael Douglas and Catherine Zeta-Jones are taking 'time apart to work on their marriage'. That's like saying they're 'staying together to explore themselves as individuals'. It's not easy making relationships with a 25-year age gap work. It must be hard for a couple to grow old together when one has such a big head start.

Keith Richards simply can't die. He's a genuine, living, pickled-and-preserved icon, talking and walking around like a sun-scorched, partially concussed half-man, with the ubiquitous Marlboro Light held in a claw-like, static, paralysed hand. A truly terrible hand. A hand that resembles an ancient, leathery, malformed foetus dry-cured in sea salt and malt vinegar.

Keith says he intimidates his daughter's boyfriends by

showing them tricks with knives. Bear in mind this is a man so off his face I'd feel intimidated standing near him while he held a hot cup of tea. His best knife trick is when he drinks a litre of Southern Comfort, and then falls face first into the cutlery drawer and manages to come up with just a teaspoon jammed into his eye socket.

Brave Angelina Jolie says her double mastectomy has brought her closer to husband Brad Pitt. By my calculations, 3.86 inches closer (granted, my model's not 100 per cent accurate – there's only so much data you can retrieve from mattress plaster casts taken after sneaking into recently vacated hotel rooms). Angelina added she doesn't want more kids. Causing jubilation across rural Cambodia, where many parents guard their huts by hanging a carving of Jennifer Aniston above the door. An impossibly sexy woman – who campaigns against war, between playing gun-toting assassins – had her breasts cut off and re-sculpted to save her own life from cancer. If her next press release could be instructions on exactly what we're allowed to masturbate about from now on, that would be very helpful, ta.

Chris Brown said in an interview that after fifty-two weeks of counselling he learned that punching a woman in the face 'is absolutely wrong'. Well done, Chris. Give yourself a peanut. Chris got a tattoo of a beaten-up woman on his neck. Contrary to what people think, it isn't a tattoo from when he beat up Rihanna – it's a flash-forward to when he kills her. What better place for your 'To do' list than on your neck. He doesn't need a tattoo to remind himself of what he did. That's what Twitter's for.

Rihanna said she can turn straight women bisexual, which I'm pretty sure was also an early advertising slogan for Lambrini. Megan Fox says her first love was a teenage lesbian stripper who broke her heart. I think she broke mine, too. Either that, or it turned me on so much I tried to grow a breast. She's having her tattoo of Marilyn Monroe removed as she says it draws negative comments. No, Megan. You misunderstand. It's your whole being that reminds people of the death of Hollywood.

Lady Gaga has given her boyfriend a scrapbook to remind him of her whenever they're apart. Surely he's reminded of her every time he looks at some raw meat, a pile of bandages or his own dick. Meanwhile, Jennifer Lopez's new lover says she has the body of a woman half her age. Though it seems that so far she's only harvested its hair and buttocks.

Why is there so much coverage of the United States over here? Most Americans struggle to recognise us on a map. Or a battlefield. Of course, the real reason that the United States is such a horror story is that they built it on top of an Indian graveyard.

Naomi Campbell advertised for a new personal assistant. Responsibilities included dry cleaning, managing her diary and dressing as a giant sycophantic talking mirror. Supermodels can be so contrary to their assistants. One minute it's 'You make me sick!'; the next it's 'You! Make me sick!'

Kelly Brook is stunned that women have sent her boyfriend Danny Cipriani sexy pictures and dirty messages. Danny is now in therapy trying to work out why he'd think looking at scantily clad women was OK while he was going out with an underwear model. I hope Sigmund Freud is available, as this one's going to take minutes. Kelly assumed that Danny had been shagging all the women he texted, showing the quaint understanding of modern life that your mum shows when she asks if you can hear her talking into her email. Kelly's a loyal girlfriend – she managed to stay with Jason Statham for seven years. I can't get through a title sequence of his films without wanting to walk out on the whole of humanity. Danny's friends claim he was bored with the relationship. Well, she would keep banging on about Syria. Why would a rugby player be so promiscuous? It's probably the inevitable subliminal effect of spending your working day chasing a giant egg.

11

PRESS

So, Lord Leveson produced his report. I enjoyed the spectacle of how boring papers started getting. Do you want to read a story about Anton du Beke getting off his bicycle? Or one where Justin Bieber's found face down in a hooker's ass? Can't we just have both in the same story?

At first, I tried to look at it from the freedom of speech angle. Steve Coogan was a cocaine-fuelled sex case. He pumped Courtney Love! Can you imagine what he'd have done if the tabloids weren't following him? They were the only thing keeping him out of jail. He'd have been like Uday Hussain. He'd have ended up getting shot by the Red Arrows when he tried to climb the Post Office Tower like fucking King Kong. It certainly made a change for Coogan to answer the question 'Can you tell me exactly what happened?' when it wasn't being shouted at him by a sobbing fiancée.

But to be honest, I feel a bit embarrassed about having been suckered in by that. None of it was about freedom of speech, unless you mean the freedom of speech of huge corporations; corporations historically opposed to freedom of speech in every other instance. People like Coogan and Hugh Grant actually did a brave thing, largely because the papers had already taken everything they could from them. It's worth remembering how few people with a career *in front* of them have spoken out about the press. They've probably made an accurate assessment of where power still lies.

Newspapers are still the real consensus-makers in Britain. They're owned directly by billionaires and conglomerates, so the views of the ruling class are straightforwardly presented. The real debate around Leveson should have been about breaking up the power of media barons by assuring as wide an ownership as possible. There was no political will to do that because politicians and media owners have very similar interests: serving power.

I've sort of been able to watch all this from the hallway, always having written columns and done interviews with a variety of newspapers. You see what does and doesn't get printed. The last five years or so have been a time of increasing conformity. News stories are presented to us differently now. During the Occupy movement, just like with the eviction of travellers from Dale Farm, we were presented with no characters – and actually almost no images of the protest – making it very difficult for the story to progress into other areas of the culture. You don't get characters from the counterculture anymore. No Swampy the environmental protester, nothing that can 'monologue', that hideous American verb of the comedian as meme processor and cultural drip tray.

I genuinely worry that Leveson will result in the press being forcibly beaten back into some kind of relevance just as their circulations are dying. Can you imagine that a teenager nowadays who's grown up with broadband is going to end up forking out for a hard copy of tits and jingoism? Even the language of the tabloids must sound to young ears like some desperate holiday rep at the last place you ever let your parents take you. We should encourage everything that is worst in the press and let them drown in their own hate. Don't ban Page 3. The men of Britain need something to hang on to. And it's knowing that in exchange for £150 their daughter might someday show her tits to every builder in the United Kingdom. That's terrifying. Which is why I go to my daughter's parents' nights, I watch her crappy plays and I praise her terrible drawings. It keeps her self-esteem up. And it makes me try to be the best father I can be. Page 3 is the mortar that holds this country's families together.

• • •

I feel it's a bit pointless to list the ways in which our culture is dead. A bit like a coroner at an autopsy documenting into the microphone, 'He's not blinking . . . he's not talking . . . he's not wriggling his toes . . . he's not clicking his fingers . . .' But here's one you might not have noticed. There's a general magazine dynamic that has got a hold of everything like gangrene. What I mean by that is that much of what we see and read now is produced to order rather than as an attempt to communicate felt experience.

Nowadays, rather than someone writing a book about China because they were obsessed with the East and travelled there, we are confronted with celebrities who go to China because they were asked to by a TV channel. And rather than giving us their impressions of what they happen to find, they're led through a variety of situations set up by their production company. We've moved from a culture of people attempting to communicate something to a culture of people who are happy to communicate anything.

It really is everywhere, this notion of working to a predetermined brief. Panel-show comedians are told which topics to cover, and journalists travel with politicians in their buses during election time, still not seeing themselves as embedded even when the seat of a chemical toilet is still warm from the prime minister's visit. You'll have noticed that you sometimes get left-field people allowed into news studios to comment on tomorrow's papers, mainly because the agenda is so rigidly set by what the papers cover.

The effect is to make it look like a lot of clever people *are interested in this shit*. They're not. The celeb doesn't give a deep-fried fuck about China, because by the very nature of being famous enough to front the show he's being torn away from his golden house, beautiful wife and the sentient robot from *Rocky III*. The comedians don't want to make jokes about the fact it was raining at the golf; they have their own interests, although to be fair nobody would want to watch a panel show where everybody talked about how much they hate other comedians. So we all desperately chatter about ever more irrelevant topics even as the world ends, having been told to write a symphony about the wallpaper in a burning building.

We think of ourselves as a society of freedom of expression but the more mainstream you go, the narrower the parameters. In live broadcasting, any time they venture beyond platitudes you can actually hear the caution. When a newsflash comes in, the average local radio DJ starts choosing her words as if she's talking a suicide off a windowsill. Of course, people will claim that nobody tells them what to say but that's because they colour in between the lines. *You say what you like if they like what you say.*

We've this constant reinforcement of what can and can't be expressed because it functions as social control. Here's a funny wee example. I was asked to do a questionnaire by the *Guardian*. They sent me a bunch of questions and there's no way I expected everything to go in. Here's how it was when I sent it in:

1. When were you happiest?
   Between Richard Hammond's high-speed car crash and receiving the news he'd survived.

2. What is your greatest fear?
   Developing locked-in syndrome at the start of *Alan Carr's Chatty Man*, then after exactly an hour falling sideways onto the remote control, switching the telly to Channel 4+1. Then when my wife comes in to hold a mirror over my face to see if I'm still breathing, I see that I'm Justin Lee Collins.

3. **What is your earliest memory?**
   Being told to kill David Cameron, then myself, about two weeks ago.

4. **Which living person do you most admire and why?**
   Colin Stagg, for obvious reasons.

5. **What is the trait you most deplore in yourself?**
   My slapdash

6. **What is the trait you most deplore in others?**
   Does being Jessie J count as a trait?

7. **What was your most embarrassing moment?**
   My son introducing me to his nursery teacher with 'He sleeps through the day!'

8. **Aside from a property, what's the most expensive thing you've ever bought?**
   Ulrika Jonsson's silence.

9. **Where would you like to live?**
   New York. I've never been there, but I know all about it from the TV. I will run a deli and date lots of women at once and be murdered in an alley by some punks.

10. **What would your super power be?**
    Invisibility. I'd kick a mime artist to death so he died with everybody thinking he was great at his job. Or I'd paint my dick to look like a Jaffa mini roll and hang around a bulimia seminar.

11. **What makes you unhappy?**
    That takes two good ecstasy.

12. **What do you most dislike about your appearance?**
    My beard, but there's absolutely nothing I can do about it.

13. **If you could bring something extinct back to life, what would you choose?**
Stewart Lee's sense of humour.

14. **What is your favourite smell?**
Beads burning in a freshly crashed car.

15. **What is your favourite word?**
Toboggan.

16. **What is your favourite book?**
The Book of the New Sun by Gene Wolfe.

17. **What would you most like to wear to a costume party?**
Katherine Jenkins.

18. **What is the worst thing anyone's ever said to you?**
Are you Frankie Boyle?

19. **Is it better to give or to receive?**
Depends what it is. Toaster – receive. AIDS – give.

20. **What is your guiltiest pleasure?**
Colin Stagg's *100 Football Howlers*.

21. **What do you owe your parents?**
Realistically, about five grand of babysitting money.

22. **To whom would you most like to say sorry and why?**
Colin Stagg. It wouldn't have helped if I'd confessed.

23. **What or who is the greatest love of your life?**
My kids. I think kids deliver on all the stuff romantic love only promises. I'm in love every day.

24. **What does love feel like?**
It feels like a belt around my throat.

25. Have you ever said 'I love you' without meaning it?
    Only to my kids.

26. Who would you invite to your dream dinner party?
    People always say Muhammad Ali, but in reality it would be horrible watching him trying to eat.

27. Which words or phrases do you most overuse?
    She was like that when I got here, Colin and Stagg.

28. What is the worst job you've ever done?
    I was fucking shit on *QI* for a few series. Oh no, hang on, that was Alan Davies.

29. If you could edit your past, what would you change?
    I'd do it all again in a funky yellow cape

30. If you could go back in time, where would you go?
    Well, obviously I'd set out to kill Hitler and get sidetracked trying to fuck the young Diana Rigg.

31. How do you relax?
    Same as everybody else, really. Looking at blueprints of the Olympic Village, digging a tunnel, dressing up as a member of Olympic Security, fucking a life-size clay model of Jessica Ennis.

32. How often do you have sex?
    I regularly have sex with someone I hate, or masturbation as I call it.

33. What is the closest you've ever come to death?
    Middlesbrough.

34. What do you consider your greatest achievement?
    You're kidding, right?

35. What song would you like played at your funeral?
   'If You Don't Know Me by Now'.

36. How would you like to be remembered?
   As a G.

37. What is the most important lesson life has taught you?
   People hate jokes.

38. Where would you most like to be right now?
   Having a heart attack in Jessica Ennis's arsehole.

What's interesting is that we all know exactly what went in and what didn't. You're right: Colin Stagg, Muhammad Ali, my borderline personality disorder sexual intentions towards heptathletes, drugs, Alan Davies – all gone. Decisions we imagine are about whether a subeditor happens to be in a good mood are actually about something else. An internalised template we've all been given about what people can and can't hear.

I will say this about the press, though. At least they always keep things in perspective. In fact I quite enjoyed the *Daily Express*'s prediction for 2025, where from coast to coast we're living like pencils stuffed in a mug, the fortunate ones being nudged off our cliffs like coins on a penny falls, only the tallest escaping permanent befoulment from their neighbour's farts, where the lottery prize will be the blissful release of a bullet from the helicopter gunships that permanently hover overhead.

12

SCIENCE

When I did stand-up I was always very conscious of when a show needed a 'dip', a lowering of energy. And often I liked to plough on regardless, just to see what would happen. Usually it would fuck the show up, but not for me really, as I'd get home quicker. You're well into the second half of the book by now and you're probably feeling that you've had enough gags for a bit. That's how I feel writing it, so let's have a wee change of pace. I've always been interested in what I suppose I'd call the pitfalls of rationality: the little reality tunnels we live in, the way rationality can cut us off from a more magical view of the world. So the introduction to this chapter is a sensible little essay about that, then we're back to daft jokes about things scientists have been up to.

Peruse the letters pages of a broadsheet newspaper and you'll gain the impression that the battle for the soul of humanity is currently being fought between the forces of science and those who value religion or who are sceptical about the benefits of modernity. It's not difficult to see parallels between many in the Richard Dawkins/secularism camp and fundamentalist religious types. What seems to unite them both is certainty.

Certainty about the nature of reality is something you won't necessarily find in the hallways and cafeterias of scientific institutions. Scratch the average Nobel Prize winner and you'll probably find someone fretting about the inexplicability of things. Stephen Hawking, for example, has publicly mused that science might soon have to abandon its quest for a 'unified theory of everything', such are the difficulties with the current picture. So what do Dawkins and his ilk know to justify their conviction and their arrogance?

There's no denying the achievements of science. A hundred years ago there were no smartphones or space stations. But what's not mentioned is the cost of technological progress. Life isn't necessarily getting better. For every new kid who's now able to plug himself into the internet, there's a little cloud of black smoke going up somewhere. In the 70s we were told to prepare ourselves for a new world of technologically supported leisure and extended free time. What we got was call centres.

The world is becoming an increasingly soulless place. We've replaced genuine human emotions with the communal buzz of the electronically connected hive mind, with its indistinguishable identikit opinions about films and TV programmes we probably won't have time to see anyway. We've substituted genuine wonder at the mystery and beauty of nature with a belief that trees and butterflies and human consciousness are machine-like.

The problem could be one of 'literalism', something that philosopher Patrick Harpur believes began to creep into humanity's thinking alongside the rise of science four hundred years ago. Nowadays, we're inclined to see the world in more concrete, narrowly defined terms than the metaphor-rich, mythic way of thinking that characterised peoples of earlier times. If nature is simply an inert assemblage of atoms, which form DNA molecules and proteins, which in turn determine the shapes and properties of plants and animals – if this is literally all it is – then it's easier to view it as expendable and less worth caring about.

This debate's not all new, either. Romanticism was born out of a deep scepticism about the Enlightenment. What came with science and the Enlightenment seems to have been something called the 'rational ego'. We began to draw boundaries around things, to say 'this is my land, not yours'.

We became preoccupied with categories and labels, with numerical quantities. Our concern with qualities such as size and number seems to have run parallel with the inflation of the human ego. Tyrants were able to quantify their own importance in terms of the size of their palaces or the amount of land they lorded over.

When you look at what human activity is doing to the planet and to human societies, it's almost possible to see the modern rational ego as a kind of cancer. Our ability to marvel at the sleek design of an iPhone is in direct proportion to our tendency to shut ourselves off from the systematic assault on the natural world that is involved in its manufacture. The modern, rational ego is greedy and exploitative. Its technologies are destroying the planet. It cuts us off from nature and from each other.

Look under the surface of a new atheist and you'll probably find someone who believes in the ultimate reality of the physical world. In fact, most of us probably have this belief nowadays, or if we don't we'll keep quiet about it when we're at work or somewhere like that, so as not to appear flaky. Nature is at its heart nothing more mysterious than the interaction of atomic particles governed by natural forces such as electromagnetism, or so the materialist story goes. It will eventually be revealed that everything from a beaver's choice of habitat to the quizzical slant of Richard Dawkins's left eyebrow is explicable in terms of physics and chemistry.

One of the areas in which this materialist slant is being called into question quite publicly is mental illness. At the time of writing, prominent academics in the world of clinical psychology were urging their colleagues to abandon the tendency to see mental-health problems as having primarily biological causes, to see patients as meaningless bundles of cells governed by the laws of chemistry. Instead, they seemed to be saying, a greater premium should be placed on understanding people's personal stories, what has happened to them, and so on.

For all that Dawkins *et al.* undermine religion because of the difficulties in establishing its literal truth, the fact is that until three hundred years or so ago nobody valued religious writings for their literal truth, but for their power as myth.

Myths have a certain quality of timelessness, of being about things that didn't necessarily happen in AD 33 or whenever, but which have always been happening – and are still happening. Whether you can be bothered with them or not isn't really the point. Myths seem to have sustained people through the strangeness and difficulties of life over several millennia. And they've obviously worked for some, as many of these stories remain with us.

The literal interpretation of things also tends to discount the weirder end of human experience. And fair enough – the people who claim to have been abducted by UFOs or to have seen a vision of the Virgin Mary in a bowl of Rice Krispies might well be nuts. But what about the experiences of visionaries and poets?

A scientific rationalist would probably see a visionary like William Blake as simply crazy. He would attempt to take his visions literally, and so scorn them as delusional. Modern culture, with its science-influenced assumptions about the nature of things, keeps us locked into a world-view where the things we experience are considered to be either subjective or objective. In other words, they're either 'all in your head' or 'all out there in the so-called "real world"'. But philosophers and psychologists acknowledge that our perceptions involve a combination of both. There's a mystical quality to the way we see the world. We don't simply see it as it is, but by means of a sensory and conceptual apparatus conditioned by the cultural context of our upbringing and life so far. And so *all* perception is really a collaboration between what's 'out there' and what's 'in here'.

Blake's vision of the sun as a company of angels was clearly as much created as perceived. We assume our science-informed view of the sun as a nuclear furnace is more accurate and useful. Blake, on the other hand, would probably have viewed this literalistic interpretation of things as soulless and just as mad in a different way.

Built into the secular world-view seems to be a belief in the idea of progress, that science is allowing us to build a better world, and that utopia lies ahead (especially if we can get rid of all these religious, irrational types holding things back). Philosopher John Gray sees in this salvation-through-scientific-progress faith an echo of Christianity, and the idea that human life can be made cumulatively better until we arrive at something akin to perfection. The idea of salvation as a historical event doesn't hold up in the face of reality, he says, explaining that improvements in human life are not cumulative in the same way that scientific advances are. Throughout history these kinds of apocalyptic faiths have tended to flounder, often leaving a huge amount of destruction in their wake. Most recently, the belief that globalisation and free-market capitalism constituted the end of history and the final triumph of Western liberal democracy looks to have been woefully over-optimistic, and is implicated in Bush and Blair's ill-fated Iraq adventure.

The idea of progress also relies on our belief in the idea of linear time, something that could itself be considered a kind of modern-day myth, an idea explored in fiction by writers such as J. G. Ballard and William Burroughs. We tend to view our lives as progressing from the past into the future like a kind of scenic railway. But this is nothing more than an idea, a construct of our imaginations. We view the present moment as something that's developed out of what's happened in the past and which derives its meaning from what we think it will lead to in the future. But this is a process that's all in our heads. For one thing, at the subatomic level, physicists have long abandoned assumptions of causality and of a linear time flowing from point A to point B.

Maybe our hopes for the future could be invested in a return to a more mythic and magical – and less literal – view of reality. While the rational, scientific mind has made huge strides in terms of our mastery of the physical world, there's room to question whether its fruits truly constitute 'progress' when you look at the problems it also seems to be helping to create: the destruction of the ecosystem, and the epidemic of depression and discouragement that seems to be taking hold throughout the Western world.

● ● ●

Several candidates have been put forward as the world's seven billionth person. Of course, the figure seven billion is just human beings and doesn't include the army that China has cloned from Jango Fett. It's amazing that seven billion people have been born and yet there's not one who's a delivery man willing to say what time he's going to come to your house.

One of the world's leading geneticists is looking for a female volunteer to give birth to a Neanderthal baby. I'm not sure what he'll end up creating, other than a cracking football team. After growing the Neanderthal embryo in a lab it will then be implanted into the volunteer's womb. I think that when it comes to volunteering most women would rather do a week in a Sue Ryder shop.

There were calls for a law that would enable children to be told if they were conceived by sperm donation. It's only fair to mention I'm the result of sperm from an anonymous donor. My mother can't reveal his identity – all she knows for sure is that it said VW on the key ring.

IVF babies could soon be created using DNA from three people, a process pioneered not just in the lab, but in lay-bys around the country. Critics say it'll demean the process of human reproduction. Having caught myself in the mirror during sex I can't imagine that's actually possible. To put it bluntly, I look like a beached manatee that's been fitted with a misfiring pacemaker.

Two men in the United States with HIV have been cured by a bone-marrow transplant. I've known for a long time that bone marrow's the key to eradicating the disease; my dogs have been eating it for years and none of them have at any point shown any symptoms of AIDS. If this proves anything it's that scraping the marrow from a healthy person and then injecting it into your own bones in an expensive, complex and life-threatening operation does seem a fair-enough price to pay to get a bareback ride off a stranger.

Scientists have used sheep cells and a 3D printer to create a human ear. Think of the potential. Have them grafted on all over your body and you could be the ultimate glasses stand in a Vision Express. People might think you look stupid bedecked with ears, but I bet they wouldn't risk bitching about you. Well, not within a hundred yards.

Scientists claim that Viagra could help men lose weight. I suppose it does make it much harder for them to get near the dinner table. For women it has the opposite effect, as men taking Viagra are no longer that bothered about what they look like. Viagra is currently used by some obese men – to help them locate the tip when they need a wee. I can see how Viagra might help you lose weight; you really do want to spend as little time as possible in a sweetie shop with a raging boner.

Scientists say that looking at Page 3 girls can speed up your mental reactions. It certainly does whenever your partner comes into the room. What this study shows us is that scientists, if given enough time and resources, will always find a way to look at naked women.

Scientists have also been trying to discover the evolutionary advantages of our fingertips becoming wrinkled when wet. I thought it would be obvious – to be a better lover. I know I always submerge my hands in a bowl of warm water for at least two hours before foreplay so my fingers become ribbed for her pleasure.

If I don't have two hours spare and need to initiate foreplay in an emergency situation a passable subterfuge is to skewer a dried apricot on to each finger. This also comes in useful if you don't want your fingerprints to be left on the body. Her body. Her living, breathing body. At least, it was when I left her apartment, Your Honour. In addition, the apricots can be a useful source of sustenance should you become victim to a countrywide manhunt.

Experts predict that in five million years men will be extinct. I don't think men will ever go extinct. Creatures become extinct because they fail to breed. Even the last man on earth would find a way to fuck himself. Human sperm could be grown in a lab to counter falling male fertility, which is partly due to female oestrogenic contraceptives finding their way into the water supply. I've been doing what I can to redress the balance by going round wanking into reservoirs.

Meanwhile, the Astronomer Royal, Lord Rees, has warned that humanity could wipe itself out by 2100. That's a bit pessimistic. I'm going for 2050. The United Nations reckons that global food shortages mean we need to start eating insects. Of course, there are pros and cons. Yes, there's not much meat on a centipede, but at least you know everyone's going to get a leg. I've been devising a snack bar that actually uses maggots as a tasty, nutritious filling. It resembles a Bounty when cut, hence my slogan – 'A Taste of Parasites'. I tried an insect diet. I had some caterpillars, and a month or so later the prospect of eating more insects filled me with a mix of excitement and nervous anticipation that there is sadly no expression for.

A Dutch lab has created beef from stem cells. It sounds frivolous, but making burgers like this might be the only way to get most American voters to ever accept stem-cell research. The researchers produced a mince-like substance, although by all accounts it takes just a simple tweak to make sausages, by swapping the beaker for a test tube. It's highly significant news for the UK, as by 2020 the demand for talent-show contestants is predicted to be so high it'll be impossible to generate enough naturally.

Stem cells could cure cancer, diabetes, autism and Alzheimer's. I like the attitude of any scientist who thinks, 'Fuck that. Get those stem cells in a bun and find me a pickle.' A hundred years from now scientists will come up with a solution to the problems of producing beef in a laboratory when someone discovers that dead cow meat makes an almost convincing substitute.

A man has been given a face transplant and regained his sense of smell. Which isn't the best time for that to return, considering all he can smell is the smoky barbecue wafts of a dead man's flesh that's been soldered on to his own skull. Another guy had the world's first successful hand transplant. A hand transplant! Imagine that. It would always feel like someone else was doing it – a dead man. If he wanks someone else off he'll technically just be watching.

A woman has had a £10,000 prosthetic tail made so she can work as a full-time mermaid. And people say there are no jobs out there. Even better was the story of the guy who had his injured penis rebuilt out of the tissue from his arm. They managed to make it look just like a real penis, apart from the tattoo reading 'MUM'. If you had an arm and hand for a penis, at the moment of climax you could high five her uterus. It would be pretty romantic if you could use your own wedding ring as a cock ring. A hand penis would come in so useful. But I'd probably end up on a register after using it to hold my pint when playing pool.

• • •

Iran successfully sent a monkey into space – and it returned safely. It's amazing, isn't it? In Iran they won't let women drive with a non-relative yet they're happy for a monkey to pilot a spaceship. In fact, I wouldn't be surprised if they didn't send a woman up first and when she survived considered it safe enough to risk a monkey. The monkey's fine and has shown no side-effects from flying into space – or at least that's what he said on his Twitter site. Iran now hopes to be able to send a monkey to the moon by 2025.

The latest Mars Exploration rover, *Curiosity*, arrived safely on the red planet. Well, it beamed back a black and white photo of some gravel, so that's all the proof I need. They say the Mars Reconnaissance Orbiter probe has used unprecedented technology – greater even than that used to pretend they landed on the moon. It'd be ironic if they did discover life on Mars squashed underneath the tyres of one of the rovers.

It's not like the pioneering days of space. It's hard to get excited when you know there isn't a bewildered monkey up there staring out at the stars thinking, 'The monkey God must be angry with me.' After all, there are a dozen metal tubes still in orbit with skeletal canine jaws clamped shut on a long-dry perished rubber feeding teat. It seems unfair they never brought them back. But, alas, it happened long before the days of the retractable lead.

It'll be a nearly a decade before a manned mission to Mars. A three-month trip, but I suspect first in the queue to go would be our Cheryl Cole, once she realises Mars's low grav-itational pull would quarter her weight and she'd be on TV

24/7. Although I'd hate to think of her shivering in the landing craft when the water teat runs dry, looking at the stars and thinking, 'The Cheryl Cole God must be angry with me.'

Scientists will first have to perfect turning urine into water. Tricky, though I've got away with passing it off as whisky when refilling a hotel minibar. The man behind the Mars space programme is Dennis Tito, who paid $20 million to the Russians in 2001 to be sent into space and who to this day holds the record for the longest period anyone's spent being jiggled about in a blacked-out caravan in the car park of a Moscow Halfords.

There's also talk that the European Space Agency is to mount a €1 billion mission to Jupiter. It would make more sense if Europe were going to Jupiter on a mission to try and find €1 billion.

No doubt these trips into space are to find other life forms to enslave. UFO expert David Clarke has argued that with so many camera phones around these days if there were any aliens on earth we'd definitely have had some good footage by now. I wish I'd read his comments earlier as I might have put up a bit more resistance to being anally probed on Tuesday night. Yes, we can all be wise after the event, and yes, in the cold light of day it was clearly more caravan than mothership. I did wonder at the time why a creature from another world would keep stopping to take orders for burgers and tea.

Sony has unveiled a mobile phone that works underwater. Which to me sounds like they've invented a new way for perverts to end up in court after they accidentally leave the HD video running and drop the phone into the ladies' toilets.

That's the thing about Sony – they've really got their finger on the pulse of the international snorkelling community. I suppose a phone that can be used underwater would come in handy for the contestants of *Splash!* to phone their agent.

Super HD is on the way, with four times the definition of standard HD. Celebs are wary, not least Simon Cowell, as he believes it might lead to his enemies discovering the one ventilation duct in his hide through which they could get a missile into his interior.

There's a new sat nav being developed especially for the elderly, although the trials haven't been problem-free. It appears that most elderly drivers insist on unplugging it whenever they stop at lights. Is it safe for an elderly relative to continue risking life and limb on the roads? Well, you'll need to have a look at their will to answer that.

Sussex Police are actually going to tag dementia sufferers who wander off. We did that with my nan. Now with just a simple tracker we can tell exactly when it's time to hide behind the sofa and pretend to be out. It would be fun to 'borrow' one, take them to Paris and straight back on the train, then drop them off outside the front door of their care home with their hair frizzed up and wearing a cape.

Talking of flying, Austrian Felix Baumgartner reached 833 mph on a sky dive. It was the most-watched live-streaming event ever on YouTube as millions of people tuned in to see one man spiral violently to his death. Imagine how many more YouTube viewers he could have achieved if he'd been serenaded by a cat playing 'Gangnam Style' on a keyboard as he landed. I couldn't watch the descent – I was too worried his 'chute would fail and he'd nut the ground, cracking open the planet to reveal the monstrous two-headed bird that surely lurks within, which would have meant I'd miss that *Bake Off* final. It's dangerous going up that high, though. There's always the risk you'll get inseminated by aliens. That could really screw his forthcoming wedding. The vicar says, 'If any of you know any reason in law why they may not marry each other you are to declare it', then Baumgartner's head slowly opens and a giant shrimp climbs out.

Baumgartner had a camera on his helmet so you could see what he was up to all of the time. What a pity Radio 1 didn't have the same policy with their DJs in the 80s. Baumgartner was protected from exposure to the outside world by his weird foil suit. In many ways, much like Jimmy Savile.

They're considering re-doing the stunt with Britain's fattest teenager to see if they can knock the earth into another solar system in a game of intergalactic billiards. Experts have warned kids not to buy a hot-air balloon, spend forty grand on helium, twelve grand on a spacesuit and jump out when the balloon's twenty-four miles up in the air – at home; although there's talk of banning helium balloons because of a shortage of the precious gas. I find you can get the same results by using normal air instead, and simply holding all your kids' parties underwater. They were a must at my son's fifth. To be honest, by the end he'd drunk so much the ones tied to his collar were all that was keeping him up.

There was an embarrassing moment at the end of Baumgartner's descent when he landed in next door's garden and they had to ring the doorbell to ask to get him back. He survived plummeting to earth at over 800 mph – which tells us Jeremy Clarkson needs to seriously rethink how fast he gets Hammond's car going on the next series of *Top Gear* to make absolutely sure he doesn't come back.

13

CRIME

You know those 'startled straight' programmes you get where prisoners visit schools to warn children of the dangers of a life of crime? You could do that with pretty much anything. Have a married guy come and talk to them. Or just somebody with a job. Try taking a weeping toddler round a shopping centre and tell me you wouldn't trade that for the excitement of bench-pressing three hundred kilos and thinking of ways to booby trap your own arsehole because you only had six weeks till someone called Mr Bojangles got out of the Infirmary?

Our whole society is founded on and fuelled by crime, and our middle and upper orders project their own vice onto those below them. The people angriest about benefit cheats are screwing their taxes; the people most concerned about Muslim violence are the ones who support blowing up Muslims in other countries; Batman thumps starving men as they try to hustle up their mortgages to Wayne Enterprise Housing Division.

Indeed, in our hearts we are all vicious criminals. Every film we make depicts the correct response to a drab job as being a bank heist; the reflex reaction to being wronged or threatened is to unleash a wave of violence/domestic terrorism. And who would watch if it were not? Liam Neeson's frustration when trying to encourage embassy officials to look into his daughter's disappearance doesn't even sound like a film. Maybe he could start killing them till they did as he said. And then the ambassador was in league with the kidnappers or something, and Liam screamed and threw him out of a window into some kind of industrial furnace.

Theresa May introduced new crime prevention injunctions, which means violent thugs can get punished without being given criminal records. A bad move, as bouncers are going to have nothing to put on their CVs. The Tories also announced that we can now beat up burglars. Thank God! I can finally let that poor man out of my basement and give him the kicking he deserves. But the Tories are yet to clarify whether it's OK – should your victim manage to crawl weakly out of your front door – to comically pull him back in by his feet and continue the punishment.

Now that you're allowed to use 'proportionate force', being burgled is probably Justin Lee Collins's best hope of forming a new relationship. In a shocking piece of news, Justin was found guilty. Surprisingly, not for crimes against TV comedy. He was given 140 hours of unpaid work – the best offer his agent will get him in the next five years. His ex-girlfriend recorded his awful rantings, although, to be fair, so did Channel 4 for many years. Justin forced his girlfriend to sleep facing him. I imagine every night she dreamed she was in an abusive relationship with a barber's floor. If being a hopeless cunt were a crime, he'd have got longer behind bars than Ian Huntley.

These revelations have changed the way I think about Justin. Now I hate him for different reasons. Claims this damaging can ruin a person's career, but fortunately for him he's already taken care of that himself. In his heyday he was often referred to as a 'loveable funnyman', then soon after just 'loveable' and now he's just known as 'man'. He made a series of shows called *Bring Back* . . ., in which he reunited the casts of old TV shows. But sadly for Justin Lee Collins, the only thing he hasn't been able to bring back to TV is Justin Lee Collins. My new favourite game is to watch *Oops TV* and do his voice over the footage of home videos going wrong, but as he'd really want to say it: 'Fallen over dancing at a wedding, have you, you dirty whore?!'

But I digress. 'Proportionate force' will probably be most exciting if you work in A&E, as for you it's going to be like you're working in a field hospital during a Viking raid. Hopefully, this law will also apply to members of your extended family that drop around unannounced.

The Tories do have other common-sense measures to reduce burglary, such as prolonging the recession to the point that few of us will still have anything worth stealing. And there's no denying the government has improved security at rural post offices – very few robbers are now prepared to invest in the petrol needed to try and find one. Thousands of police officers are to be sacked and hundreds of police stations replaced with public-contact points in supermarkets. At least those who've kept keep their jobs can keep in touch with those who haven't, as most will be tailing old ladies they think have hidden frozen chickens under their hats. Fewer police just has to affect response times. I bet we'll now have to wait ages before they turn up to tell us there's not really anything they can do. Police say it could mean more riots. I doubt it. Not with all the effort that's been put in since the last ones to tackle inequality.

Forty per cent of female police officers consider quitting on account of low morale. I suppose not many things can be as depressing as having all the hassle of being in the police without the physical strength to cheer yourself up by barging an old man with heart problems to his death. Of course, it's ludicrous to suggest PC Simon Harwood got off lightly for his attack on Ian Tomlinson. I believe he might yet be charged with wilfully damaging a baton.

The Met claimed they will save £300 million by closing sixty-five police stations. Officers will be moved into post offices, which could save on squad car costs, too, as officers will be able to cover themselves in stamps, write the crime-scene address across their chests and then just climb into a sack – which might have another benefit of a much-needed reduction in response times.

The government is to get tough on soft-touch jails. I agree that they're becoming increasingly like holiday camps, as pretty soon they'll all have their own washed-up 70s and

80s TV entertainers . . . and there are a few in Northern Ireland that could hold their own in any knobbly-knees contest. I'm not surprised prisoners sit around every day watching *Jeremy Kyle*. To be fair, it's the only way they get to see their families. Of course prisoners are going to watch TV all day. What do they want them to do? Go on a tour of the National Gallery?

Should prisoners be allowed to vote? Surely the real question here is whether we can trust them to come back from the polling station. The UK's blanket ban on prisoners voting has been found to be a breach of human rights, a very popular decision with the nonce wing, who are extremely excited at the prospect of visiting a primary school once every four years. We shouldn't be governed by people in Strasbourg with no popular mandate. That's the job of people in London with no popular mandate.

This'll mean political parties will have to appeal to prisoners, too – Labour might win the next election on the promise to reduce the price of a bumming to one fruit and nut bar. I really don't want to live in a country where a cake being brought into prison is used to smuggle a laminated copy of the Liberal Democrat manifesto. Politicians will have to take on prisoners' ideas – like the best thing to do with the euro is put a load in a sock and hit a nonce in the eye with it. The criminally insane still won't be allowed to vote, however, so the Lib Dems won't benefit from the move.

Why not let psychopaths and mass murderers vote? After all, we've been voting for them for years. Perhaps the vote should only be for people serving short sentences – somehow

I don't think a lifer is really going to take the need for a new lollipop lady in Chiswick that seriously. Politicians will now have to canvass in prisons – and I'm guessing unless any of them are standing on an 'Allow men to hide in bushes and follow women' ticket, most will be leaving the beast wing with a 'Don't know'. I know who most rapists will be voting for: the Green Party. Their policy of more parkland in urban areas and dimming street lights to save energy is a rapists' charter.

●　　●　　●

Prisoners having sex changes in UK jails will be allowed to buy padded bras and make-up. And why not? Who doesn't want to look their best as they're slopping out or being savagely beaten with a sock filled with snooker balls? No matter how feminine they look, I can't help feeling the fact they're in a male prison is a bit of a giveaway.

A sex change didn't help notorious Colombian gang member Giovanni Rebolledo, who was arrested despite having the operation and working as a prostitute. Hiding from the police dressed as a prostitute makes about as much sense as hiding from the police disguised as a giant doughnut. He thought they would never suspect him if he had a sex change, but there's only one foolproof way to avoid detection by the police and that's to have been on British TV in the 70s.

A £9 million nationwide database is being established to identify children who might be at risk of abuse. The project is simply to digitise every letter sent to *Jim'll Fix It*. Speaking of which, former *This Morning* stalwart Fred Talbot has got people talking about the weather again. The whether or not he's a paedophile.

Police have revealed that Cyril Smith did molest children. How did he lure them? You might think any kid could outrun Cyril. Not so, as tragically the children's home in question was at the top of a hill. It must have been like being sexually abused by that boulder in *Indiana Jones and the Temple of Doom*.

In retrospect, dressing like a PE teacher should have been bit of a giveaway that Savile was a paedophile. With his badges and TV show to make dreams come true, other paedophiles' bags of sweets paled by comparison. 'I can make their dream of eating their lunch on a roller coaster come true – what've you got? A Transit van and a packet of Mentos? Fuck off!' When you think about it, Savile had a specially equipped chair with treats for kids concealed in it – it's like Ian Huntley being supplied by Q from Bond's MI6.

We've got to remember he raised a lot of money for charity and some of that must have gone to his victims. It's sick he raised money for that MRI machine at Stoke Mandeville. Bad enough wanting to see kids naked, let alone without their skin and soft tissue, too.

Hats off to the BBC, though. After a mere thirty-five years they leapt into action, saying they'd cooperate with any police enquiry. The channel apparently made Savile wear all that jewellery so kids would hear him coming, the same way you'd put a bell on a cat. After all this, maybe the BBC will have to take action on rumours. Like, for example, the ones I'm starting about Richard Hammond shagging monkeys.

In order to save time, the police are now advising that only women who were not abused by the paedophile Tarzan should phone in. Savile has achieved the impossible – a further tarnishing of the image of the nylon shell suit. Euugheeeuuurgheeuuurgh! That was one of his catchphrases. Cynically making it like his cum-noise so no one would bat an eyelid hearing it through his dressing-room door.

I actually felt quite emotional when I heard. I can't tell you how much I love not having to pay someone I've sponsored to do the marathon. He was a great friend of royalty, business and the Church. As I found out when he fixed it for me to be abused on an altar by some giant lizards and their lion-headed archmage, Dr Pandemonium.

Is the sex offenders' register now just an old copy of the *Radio Times*? Pretty weird to think that the only guy in entertainment who wasn't a sex criminal was Benny Hill. It explains why teenagers' fashions and hairstyles were so bad in the 70s, as making yourself unattractive was the best means of defence against show-business personalities.

• • •

The government's made stalking a criminal offence, which should help ensure it's even more exciting. It's now punishable by up to five years in prison. This is great news, as I really need an incentive to quit. They'll be able to put away the nutcase who's watching Natasha Kaplinsky's house from that other bush. I know Tash is worried about him – she tells me while reading the news, using our special blinking code.

If found guilty, two young women face eight years in Peruvian jail being played like the pan pipes. The British girls, who were arrested in Peru, have handed a list to their family. It included a variety of items including Pringles, hair-removal cream, Nutella, a pack of cards, cornflakes and a bra. There's only one man capable of collecting the items in times of crisis. Step up to the plate, Mr Paul Gascoigne. I have a theory that the whole thing's a misunderstanding and the Peruvians think the girls keep admitting to stuff, because it's tricky for a Scottish girl not to end every sentence with 'see?'

Many women were coveting Michaella Connolly's jacket. Finally something about this case that women can masturbate over as well. The case has something for everyone – sexy dancers for the dads, cool fashion for the mums, and complex legal and moral arguments for their children as yet unblunted by the horrors of daily life. I'm shocked that people are talking about Connolly's jacket. I didn't think society had got to the stage where we were printing pictures of young women in clothes. Connolly will also be asked in prison who made her jacket – but the prisoners will be asking in case it was any of their six-year-olds.

My one piece of advice when travelling? There's only one time it's worth carrying someone else's bag in an airport. After it's been round the carousel at least twice and no one's come forward.

A crazed woman broke into Simon Cowell's house with intent to inflict grievous bodily harm. She should be locked up for not managing it. She was eventually caught hiding in his wardrobe, although quite why she thought she'd run into Simon in a closet I've no idea. Deluded and mentally unstable, she was only released after guaranteeing that she'd turn up for future *Britain's Got Talent* auditions. The woman was described as a 'fan' – well, if she only wanted to smash Simon's head in with a brick then she probably liked him better than the rest of us. He described the woman brandishing a brick as being like a scene from a horror film. Which one? *Builder on Elm Street*? I'm sure we can all remember that scene in the Hitchcock film where fuck all happens.

I can't understand why she was armed with a brick. After all, just a cursory search of Simon's toilet cabinets and she could have been armed with a two-foot-long dildo with a fist on the end, similar to those used by the Syrian army. Maybe it was her audition for *BGT*, and she'd just shat the brick out. Simon was concerned that she could have had a gun. Yes, but I think you'd have had time to make an escape while she tried to load the brick into the chamber.

Simon will be ready if it happens again and will call Sinitta, just like Zeus summoning the Kraken. It seems that, when told she might face six months in prison, the intruder broke down, screaming, 'At least make it till the next *X Factor*'s over!' He's now stepping up security at his home – somehow, I'm fairly certain no women will ever get into Simon's bedroom again. Her trial was like a tense stand-off between her and a group of black teenagers who'd turned to crime to keep them out of street dancing. It must have been confusing for Simon to hear a psychiatric assessment that didn't end with the words 'fully fit to undergo a world tour'.

Fellow *X Factor* judge Tulisa Contostavlos found herself on the wrong side of the law and she was recorded admitting that she used to deal crack. It must make plugging her latest album all the more depressing when she remembers that she used to be involved in selling something people really wanted. Of course, a lot of people around her probably needed to take crack, as Dappy is a lot more tolerable if you think he's a hallucination.

I hope Tulisa doesn't go to prison, but I'm not going to lie and say the idea doesn't turn me on. Although I'd imagine that after a year of having to sit next to Louis Walsh, being muff-dived by a convicted arsonist as a pool forfeit will feel like a spa weekend. You really don't want the nickname 'The Female Boss' when the police are trying to establish how high up you are in a drug-supply chain.

In the video Tulisa said she didn't take drugs herself. I believe her; she seems like a sociable person. And if you were going to alter your mind you'd hardly settle for the one she's ended up with. Tulisa has talked of working for a crack dealer in her youth, claiming she did well because of her looks. Tulisa, if you're hanging round with crack addicts, that's a pretty low bar on the appearance front. No one really believes that Tulisa was a drug dealer – she was just trying to make herself sound more credible. It's the schemie equivalent of padding out your CV. If she were a member of Coldplay she'd be bragging to undercover reporters that's she's got Grade 5 on the bassoon and makes her own honey. Tulisa appears to have had no idea that she was being videoed, as none of the undercover reporters got their penis out.

Tulisa has given up battling for damages over her leaked sex tape to avoid racking up even more lawyers' fees, although she did manage to stop her ex from making any money from it. The irony being that if she'd let him make a few quid he'd have been able to afford to pay her the damages she was after. Her ex had hoped to make a fortune but only six people paid to see her sex tape, netting a grand total of £23. It made me quite angry, but also curious about who the other five people were.

Ken Clarke's admitted we're losing the war against drugs. Maybe it's finally time to switch sides and join them in their glorious fight against our hideous, hideous reality. Magic mushrooms are said to help combat depression. It's hard to feel sad when you're in a knife-fight with Kermit the Frog.

According to a United Nations official, drugs gangs control Manchester, Liverpool and Birmingham. It feels like a historic day when someone talks about drug problems without mentioning Glasgow. If there are so many drugs in these cities then it does beg the question why aren't the people who live there a bit more cheerful? They want to instigate drug-prevention programmes for youngsters – well, it's going to be one hell of a good youth club to be more exciting than crack. I'm proud to say that my kids would never get involved in drugs – they're far too pissed. Stories like this are so worrying that even the UN official had to spark up a spliff to take the edge off. Despite this report, it would be wrong to think of people from these cities as all being drug pushers – many of them are thieves or benefit cheats.

I don't fancy this idea of heroin addicts getting community sentences. I'd hate to think of one painting my nan's house.

She could turn nasty if they find her stash. I'd prefer speed addicts, maybe; then they'd have it done in time for *Bargain Hunt*. Mitch Winehouse is setting up a foundation in his daughter's name so he can help save young addicts. Hmm. It's not exactly an area where he's got a great track record.

Tulisa's former bandmate Dappy has been ordered to do 150 hours of community service, roughly equating to a two-month ban from the recording studio. Americans do that whole lawbreaking celeb thing on a much grander scale. A US talent agency has pitched Lindsay Lohan as 'available for bar mitzvahs'. I was going to book Lindsay for a party myself but decided to drag it upmarket and get a hooker in her place. No, only joking, I booked Michael J. Fox instead – unfortunately I gave him the job of serving the peas and I'm still finding them on top of the curtain pelmets and lampshades.

Meanwhile, *Glee* actor Cory Monteith died from an overdose of heroin and alcohol. A lesson to us all – that heroin and alcohol should only be taken in moderation. In gun-crazed America a five-year-old boy was given his own gun, which he used to shoot and kill his little sister. The boy was expected to be safe because he'd had the gun for a year. To be fair, a year ago his sister wouldn't have been as annoying. The coroner called it 'a crazy accident', showing all the logic and skills of a man who defines heart attacks as 'that little drummer in his chest got out somehow'. He'd always behaved safely when out hunting, but then deer and rabbits didn't break his Action Man. Many parents battle with teaching kids the concept of death. At least they won't have to buy him a goldfish now. Five-year-olds just don't have a concept of death, which is why they can watch the *Chipmunk* films without crying for Jason Lee's career. Things were so much simpler when I was a kid. If you wanted to kill your sister you had to go to the effort of writing a letter to *Jim'll Fix It*.

Ninety-three thousand Americans have signed a petition to have Piers Morgan extradited back to the UK for his views on gun control. Ironically, the only sane argument I have for allowing Americans to be heavily armed is that Piers Morgan lives there. I'm against the use of guns. Especially on Piers Morgan. I'd prefer something far more time-consuming if you're planning to assassinate him. Maybe a rusty melon-baller or a plastic trowel from a child's gardening set.

A plastic gun can be downloaded from the internet and made on a 3D printer. You go to print out your dissertation, hit the wrong button and print a plastic gun. Five years later you're bombing the Houses of Parliament with a plastic jet. A gun that comes out of a printer? It's bound to jam. The inventor says it doesn't violate US gun laws. As he's not been able to find any. Just because people are buying these 3D printers doesn't mean they're going to print off guns from the internet. My priority would be life-sized erotic jigsaws.

There are to be long jail sentences for selling guns to UK gangs. Quite right. These people need to realise they must either stop, or go legit, get a suit and do it in the Third World where it doesn't matter. It's hoped new laws will protect terrified members of the public from being hit by bullets flying between police, and terrified members of the public.

• • •

Notorious Moors murderer Ian Brady went on hunger strike. Careful, Ian. If you get too small and frail you'll end up wanting to torture yourself. Brady signed legal papers instructing doctors not to resuscitate him if he collapses. I understand Brady's position. I'd want to die, too, if I now looked like a perpetually quizzical Paul McCartney. Brady could stage a dramatic escape from prison if McCartney ever did a show there. Brady could walk straight out past the guards and the only questions they'd ask would be, 'What's up, Paul? Have you lost something? It looks like you're trying to remember the name of the butler in *The Fresh Prince of Bel-Air*.'

Derek Acorah said he's known Madeleine McCann's been dead for five years, but didn't want to say anything during the sensitive time that he didn't have a book out. Acorah used to present TV's *Most Haunted*, which is now just a slow close-up of Tess Daly's eyes.

It's not the first time Acorah's said something shocking. This was nothing compared with finding out that he's married with kids. I can understand why Derek speaks to the dead, as there isn't a person alive who wants to exchange a single word with the prick. Acorah has let down the entire psychic community by saying something that is statistically likely to be true. Actually, I'm very confident Maddie will be found next year, as everyone finds nine-year-olds annoying.

Making logical suppositions about a child that lack tact and upset the parents doesn't mean you're a psychic. It means you're an in-law. If you're really psychic surely you'd pick the one option out of two that wouldn't make everyone think you're an arsehole.

Kate McCann accused Acorah of being a self-publicist. At least, that's what it says on the cover of her new book. The McCanns say they're not going to listen to a deluded old bloke who claims to speak to the dead, which should save them another trip to the pope. Acorah wanted to spare the McCanns further suffering by not pointing out how much cheaper it is to fly to Portugal when you're not tied to school-holiday dates.

The Metropolitan Police like to think Maddie is still alive, because they get a better tan in Portugal without having to wear those stifling crime-scene overalls. The police have been talking to Acorah as they can't rule out any lead, especially one presented by someone who looks like a homicidal nonce. When he's possessed he looks lost and confused. If you want the experience of seeing his show, just throw £50 in a shredder and then ask your dad how to work the washing machine.

14

EDUCATION AND KIDS, YO!

Education is a key battleground because in order to function, society doesn't need you to be just a bit stupid. No, for you to subsidise a welfare state for billionaires you're going to need to be a real slack-faced fuckpuzzle. You'll have to be the sort of person who, while having both their basic liberties and their assets taken from them, would choose to focus on a thing a footballer did at a thing. Society needs you to be able to sit through a talent show that will be won by an animal. It needs you to be stupid enough to wave a little plastic flag at some cunts on a golden barge while your kid gets his legs blown off to secure an oil executive's bonus.

Maybe this need for abject cluelessness is why thousands of secondary-school pupils are now being taught by teachers who don't possess degrees in the subject they teach. Most teenagers don't need a teacher with a degree. What they really look for is a responsible grown-up who, over time, they can make have a complete mental breakdown. We shouldn't worry too much about degrees. Teaching is a vocation for most people. Teachers want to give something back, like all the misery and hate that they suffered at school.

Michael Gove wants to introduce performance-related pay in schools. That's wrong. Of course everyone hates PE teachers but we can't just let them starve. I say leave teachers alone as they have enough problems as it is. Traffic can be a nightmare at half three.

Children will be made to read fake words like 'terg', 'fape' and 'ulf' in an effort to gauge their reading levels. The bogus words will be mixed up with real words in tests. It shows how little the examiners know about popular culture, as these words are already common in text speak. Only today I sent a text hoping Danny Dyer would be viciously faped with a foot-long terg until his ulf snapped, bled and withered.

Carol Vorderman's spoken out about the importance of children's numeracy. Quite right, Carol. Otherwise they might not possess the skills to avoid having the wool pulled over their eyes by loan-consolidation outfits selling poor-quality options at a high rate of interest.

An education system should be all about the love of learning. If you can successfully crush that, you've got yourself a compliant workforce. The problem with school is that it teaches you a lot of useless stuff. For example, since I've been an adult I've never once had to fend off a randy priest. We've been sliding down the education results table too long. Not like in my day, when the only thing sliding down the table was Mr Harris, lycra pants stretched to structural limits, while we reluctantly provided an accompaniment with 'Je t'aime' played on a comb and paper.

Michael Gove also announced a 'free school' to be staffed by ex-army teachers. Nick Clegg begged Gove to only bring free schools into deprived areas. For Gove, that applies to anywhere that pasteurises its goats' cheese.

Gove's always appalled me. He's an education secretary with every quality you would hope schools would educate out of children: priggishness, ignorance and a lack of concern for other people. Even his physical appearance is something that schools usually eradicate through bullying. You can't swan around a comprehensive looking like a boggly-eyed novelty toy that when you throw it hard enough at a window sticks by its lips. You'll be – justifiably – beaten to death. If he'd gone to my school Gove would either have had to morph his body into an entirely different shape or have his sodomised corpse discovered crammed behind a boiler in a storeroom.

But getting more ex-soldiers into teaching is a great idea. Especially now all schools are obliged have disabled access. Sounds to me like it's a discount way of training up reserve troops. Child armies are good at sneaking up on the enemy, who assume they're adults that are just still in the distance. One thing's for sure. A kid's only going to push an ex-soldier too far the once! They won't want a second scene with him sobbing on the floor trying to fight the flashbacks of his mates burning in an upside-down Land Rover.

Studies show that returning soldiers take up to ten years to feel safe, not under attack and revert back to thinking that killing is wrong. I'm just not sure the middle of an urban secondary school is the place to undergo this therapy. At least kids can't say geography is boring if they're being taught by an overweight drunken man with a knife in his sock, having flashbacks whenever he discusses the mountain range where he killed three men with a radio aerial. Do teenagers need to be taught by alcoholic security guards? Surely they get enough of that at home.

A red-headed schoolboy was told he has to be taught in isolation – because he's being bullied by classmates for being ginger. They're also giving him a thirty-second head start at home time to make it sporting. The teachers have taught a very powerful lesson – it's not OK to be born different.

A ten-year-old boy started back at school as a girl. Now, first of all, if you're an adult and want to dress as the opposite sex or get a sex change, I'm all for it – it's all part of life's great parade. I just wonder, though . . . if a ten-year-old is not allowed to get a tattoo, a tongue piercing and is considered too young for make-up, should they be allowed to get a vagina? The boy and his mother have been photographed from behind and look exactly the same. It's not been reported whether she has any daughters. But I think we can guess, can't we?

Nobody makes major life decisions based on what they did at primary school. Otherwise the world would be full of virtuoso recorder players. If we're going to give ten-year-olds surgery to turn them into the person they're convinced they should be we'd better stock up on injections of radioactive spider bites.

Males are five times more likely to want gender reassignment than females. This is because men's clothes are shit.

The mother said her son started showing signs of wanting to be a girl at two and a half. How can you say a two-and-a-half-year-old shows female tendencies? I've a four-year-old boy and as far as I remember a couple of years ago he was pretty much just screaming that he hated me. So, yeah, behaving like every woman I've ever known.

I'm sure this was a hard decision for the family. I'm just not sure that the thing you are convinced of at ten should mean an irreversible life decision. I was 100 per cent convinced at ten that if I didn't switch my light on and off twice at night my mother would die. We didn't then take the next step of wiring my light switch up to her pacemaker. If British schoolchildren are going to be allowed to go to school dressed as the person they believe they are inside, I expect to see a lot of kids blacking up at the start of next term.

Experts say that sex-education lessons should start in nursery school. Well, there's at least one teacher in the UK who thinks they should begin just as the ferry leaves British waters.

Speaking of holidays, schools are to enforce fines if your kid misses lessons because of holidays. Like many parents I don't feel I've a choice. Without someone working those allotments the cabbages would be ruined while his mum and I are in Florida.

In a poor choice of phrase, David Cameron said he's planning a big shake-up of childcare. I, too, worry about the high cost of childcare. In fact, sometimes I just can't see how he's ever going to pay it all back. Of course, there's a list of babysitters prepared to work well below the market rate. Unfortunately, it's the sex offenders' register.

We're still paying the most in Europe for childcare. Not a problem for me; I relish caring for a young child. Each day starts with the swings and a play in the sandpit. Then after a couple of hours I just head home, slip him another half a tramadol as he rouses, then it's back to the park.

Grandparents do the equivalent of £7 million of babysitting. Let's not forget pensioners often have exactly the right skills to look after toddlers, as many are going deaf. One thing I can be sure of when I leave my boy with my mum is that he's not going to run off. The horizontal arms of her cruciform gravestone means there's no way he can slide his leash off the top.

● ● ●

Britain is a cosy, polite carve-up, but for anyone outside that gentlemen's club things are pretty bleak. Half a million families live in rented houses so damp it affects their health. It happened to me as a student. I ended up in hospital, as it turned out the mushrooms were poisonous.

Child poverty in the UK will soar by 2015. At least we won't have the unhappiest kids in Europe; these will be the ones whose toys have been shipped to us following a UN appeal. But there's a silver lining to every cloud – the poorer your childhood, the better sob story you'll have on the twenty-four-hour rolling death match that is *X Factor 2015*. The Tories say they don't want to trap families on benefits, so they're trapping them in poverty. The Tories also say they're cutting benefits to encourage people to get jobs, which, in the current climate, is like saying, 'We're cutting medicine to encourage you to become immortal.' Our current definition of poverty is in comparison to the expected standard of living in the UK. The Tories want to compare it globally, so we won't count a child as poor until they're floating to school on a bloated cow's carcass.

The recession means parents are no longer splashing out on expensive toys – because their children have been taken into care. I refused to dress up as Santa for my son's nursery just in case he recognised me – because of the white beard I wear to wake him every night at 3 a.m. and whisper, 'Boy! You've been asleep for FIFTY YEARS!!'

A survey revealed that most kids prefer the boxes their presents come in to the presents themselves. True for my boy. Although it could be my fault for wrapping that puppy up so far in advance. He loved that box. He crawled under it and wouldn't come out for three days.

New research shows that two in five parents won't let their children have second-hand clothes. That's ridiculous. Wearing hand-me-downs taught me a valuable lesson. If you get bullied, never run. Actually, it was damn near impossible in those heels.

Charities condemned a babygrow that had the slogan 'They shake me.' It's one of several items of clothing making light of child abuse, the most common being those with the Nike symbol on them.

In the United States a six-year-old was handcuffed and charged after having a tantrum at school. Quite right, it's the only way kids will learn. Either put your shoes on quickly or you're getting kettled. If our kids knew we owned a Taser they might put a bit more effort into those awful glitter and dried-pasta collages they turn up with. 'Daddy, it's a horse!' ZAP! 'Not good enough, baby. Not good enough.'

Should we be allowed to punish kids more severely? I don't know. Surely if it's legal it'll take away the thrill. Call me an optimist but I don't think bad classroom behaviour today means these kids will be unruly adults tomorrow. Their Chinese overlords will be able to send a few volts through their compliance caps or simply withhold their radiation meds.

Figures recently released revealed that in the last five years 1,200 kids aged seven and under have been permanently excluded. Of course, it's very easy to stop a six-year-old coming back to school. Just take him to the next street, spin him round a few times, then run away. But it's a problem that so many kids leave school with a lack of moral guidance and a reading age of eleven. Especially as the police aren't going to be recruiting any time soon. Could riots be avoided if cuts lead to fewer police? Maybe. I suppose there'd be less to get the ball rolling by shooting at the public.

Labour's David Lammy said that if parents could smack their kids the riots would never have happened. I confess, after that summer's troubles I lost control and hit my boy. I felt bad about it, but I did distinctly tell him to get size 44 Nikes. A lot of parents are worried that if they smack their kids social services will spring into action and several years later will come knocking on the door of their previous address. New research claims that hitting children gives them cancer in later life. A dilemma for me, as it's the only way I can get mine to hand over his fags.

Another study revealed that one in four kids comes close to death before the age of sixteen. The fact is you can't wrap your kids up in cotton wool, as before long they'll only get rounded up by some sick paedo with a Border collie. Don't overprotect kids. You put them in a big hamster ball and what happens? One day they suffocate because a child molester sticks his cock in the air hole.

A school banned triangular flapjacks for being too dangerous. Flapjacks are very dangerous to teens, as the roughage may finally force five years worth of fried chicken through their colons in one go.

Flapjacks being dangerous is great news, as the child soldiers of Sierra Leone can now make the weapons required to murder their own families at an after-school club. Presumably the kid who works out that you can break a square flapjack in half to make two triangular ones gets an A level and free rein of the Broadmoor kitchens.

Flapjacks have already been banned from Scottish schools for years, after it was discovered the golden liquid in the mixture wasn't actually heroin – and anyway the points always got stuck in the basket of the deep fryer.

Jamie Oliver slagged off Michael Gove for delaying improvements to school dinners. I used to get free school lunches. It was one of the many perks of bullying. The problem is that parents will still turn up at breaks with unhealthy snacks. My mum did. She was discreet, though, dressing as a cow and filling a marigold glove with syrup, before rearing up and wedging the finger teats through the railings.

Recent research shows that 20 per cent of children are obese. It's the other children I feel sorry for. That seesaw is going nowhere. In addition, the number of teenage boys with eating disorders has trebled in the past decade. Although to put a more positive spin on things, if you measure it by mass it's actually gone down.

Be sure your kids take care trick-or-treating. I always send my lad out the night before. Not only does he avoid the rush, it means I've plenty of sweets to give out on the 31st. I'm joking, of course. They all go straight into his Christmas Day shoebox. I recommend a jumbo bag of jelly babies. They're perfect for chewing on as you sit in the dark waiting for the knocking to stop. It's always difficult finding a costume that will frighten kids as soon as you open the door. This year I'm going with Y-fronts and an ankle tag.

One in five school-leavers is overweight. Surely that's just a sensible precaution, building up fat reserves for unemployment. It was estimated that there were already one million obese teenagers in the UK in 2012. Good, finally a bit of peace on the top deck of the bus. Britain is the fattest country in Europe – it seems a generation has been inspired by the Olympics to get diabetes. One in three kids is obese – although there are fears that figure might rise to one in two if the fat ones start eating the others. There is one upside to greater numbers of obese and anorexic kids – arranging them in lines could be a great hands-on way to teach binary to paedophiles.

The weight of Britain's fattest teenager – Georgia Davis – has shot up to a worrying forty-six stone. I suppose on the plus side it shows bullying has clearly gone down a bit. There are upsides to her putting all that weight on. Apparently, her order for five new pairs of knickers is all that's keeping Harland and Wolff open. Georgia has gone back into hospital after having a pain in her leg. It must be really annoying to be hospitalised by something you haven't seen for three years. She's been described as being a prisoner to her own armchair – I think you'll find the poor armchair is very much the victim in this scenario. It's not surprising that her legs are struggling – essentially you're asking a pole designed for tents to hold up a motorway flyover at rush hour.

• • •

Along with obesity, alcohol is another worrying threat to our children's health. The people of Hull were saddened to see an eleven-year-old drinking a bottle of vodka with his mum. Mourning the loss of one less bottle of vodka available in the shops. The pair were spotted arguing outside a shop. I think it was over what made the best mixer for vodka – tonic or Um Bongo. It's not typical in Hull to see mums passing cans to their kids; most of the populace have yet to discover the melding process that can bind tin to steel. Amy Johnson was from Hull. It's telling that its most famous daughter is known for risking her life to get to the other side of the world.

In a way, it makes a change to see a woman passing alcohol to her son in the fresh air rather than the traditional British method of through the placenta. The boy was said to regularly get drunk with his mother, unlike now, when he'll be regularly getting drunk with the staff of his care home. The boy's been taken into care so he'll no longer be in the grip of his mother – or any mother, considering nobody wants to adopt an eleven-year-old boy. He might be pissed, but he's the only eleven-year-old in the country who's facing being sent to an enormous building in which he will be incarcerated for five years alongside a bunch of terrifying teenagers, with a feeling of numb confidence.

Alcohol is bad for the children of Britain. It will affect their ability to adhere to Simon Cowell's touring schedule. The incident in Hull is going to be turned into a film – they're just waiting for Will Smith's kid to be addicted enough to meds to find his motivation. Joking aside, you should on no account go drinking with an eleven-year-old. They'll only get refused when it's their turn to buy a round.

Drivers caught speeding past a primary school in Merseyside were forced to either face a 'pupils' court' to explain their behaviour or have three penalty points on their licence. I know it's illegal to drink and drive but it's not illegal to be drunk when you go into a primary school to explain why you were speeding. I'd love to stand up in front of the class, drinking a can of super-strength lager, and explain that your boss is a dick and he goes mad when you turn up late, and that you can't lose the job as you're going through a divorce and need the money to pay alimony otherwise the judge will rule that you're an unfit father and you shouldn't see your children. By the time I left that school the teachers would never allow another human being into the classroom and the kids would be so on my side that they'd be asking if in technical-studies class they could be allowed to draw go-faster stripes on to the side of my car.

Nicotine is another danger to our kids, and school children as young as twelve are being given nicotine patches on the NHS without their parents' knowledge, although surely they get suspicious when their kids stop stealing their cigarettes. The problem has got so bad that kids are now sneaking to the back of the bike shed to have hypnotherapy.

Ministers announced that raunchy pop videos should carry an age warning so people can tell which ones are suitable for children. Not, as I thought, to let men know which ones are worth bothering with. I think this is great, as age ratings will let dads know when they're too old to watch a Taylor Swift video. I do agree that the likes of Katy Perry and Lady Gaga jumping about in their pants are inappropriate, although when it comes to Beyoncé and Rihanna I think I need to do a little bit more research.

Experts suggest you should watch raunchy music channels with your kids so you can add comment and context. I can't see me doing that; I feel uncomfortable enough as it is mas-turbating in front of the cat.

15

HEALTH

There was a drive recently by mental-health groups for people to stop using mental-health labels metaphorically, which was thought to trivialise serious problems. A press release from one of the organisations had a quote from a doctor about a patient's mother bursting into tears when someone said, 'The weather's being a bit schizophrenic today.' Of course, the idea that anyone could tell that woman she was over-reacting is ridiculous. I actually think that words for mental-health problems might function better as metaphors than as clinical diagnoses. Schizophrenia, OCD, autism – the kinds of words that have found their way into everyday conversation – are actually quite nebulous terms used to define disorders with wildly different symptoms. As a basic metaphor for behaviour, someone describing themselves as 'a little bit autistic' is probably a realistic way of opening up to their anal side or to their emotional blocks. It might well be helpful that people actually now identify themselves with those who have such disorders.

'Autistic' as a clinical definition of a person is quite dehumanising. It places a label on to a human being, one that can't really describe them because it covers a whole spectrum of dysfunction. Of course, this has no place in our current discourse. It's easier to be silent. Easier for whom? For some mythical normal majority? Clearly, making a word taboo unless it's used with the utmost seriousness cannot be good for those people labelled with the disorder. Why does everyone think things will improve if their issue is viewed as 'serious'? The public already probably views schizophrenia as more serious – and more negative – than it sometimes actually is. Lots of people with schizophrenia lead a perfectly normal life – even though there's no such thing. Maybe people being more light-hearted about schizophrenia, autism, Down's syndrome – whatever – would actually be better. Sure, these conditions might be part of who you are, but a schizophrenic's biggest problem at the time you meet him might well be that his football team just got beat.

Jokes have various social functions. Sometimes they're there to remind us of the hideous nature of reality, sometimes they help us to escape it. There was an interesting thing with the film *The Pirates! In an Adventure with Scientists!* It was an Aardman kids' animation and somewhere in the trailer the pirates meet a ship of lepers. There were some childish jokes about bits of lepers falling off and this sparked a spot of outrage, with some people saying it was giving kids a stereotyped, untrue view of the disease. *The Chronicles of Thomas*

Covenant starts with a writer getting leprosy and going to a sanatorium to see some sufferers. He's welcomed in to a patient's bedroom, where a kind of living stump hisses to him, 'Kill yourself! Better than this!' It takes the whole thing appropriately seriously and gives a much more clinically accurate description of late-term leprosy, but also a more damaging impression of the disease. I know, because I read that as a kid and I actually dropped the book.

Nobody's saying it's particularly helpful for *The Pirates! In an Adventure with Scientists!* to knock out a couple of cheap gags, but in that film could they have reasonably come across a ship filled with realistic late-term lepers? It would harrow an entire generation. So what's the implied alternative? Leave the lepers out. Ignore them. This is a big part of how groups are marginalised in society, right the way up to a whole sex.

My idea is that if things like leprosy are symbolically charged anyway, why not choose a way of charging them that might be more helpful? It's not very helpful to portray people's hands suddenly dropping off, but what about portraying leprosy as not a huge deal? About portraying Down's syndrome as not a huge deal? Or physical disability as not something that defines someone? Ideas and words are just symbols, and you decide what they mean. Let's go for some meanings that might actually be of some use, rather than just ignoring people. Let's update this shit to a point where it works.

What will equality look like when we get there? It surely won't look like a stultifying inability to talk to each other. It's odd that people get so wound up about people joking about a serious subject. Nobody would ever say there shouldn't be a song about rape. And rhyme is pretty trivial-ising in its own way. Two verses in, someone's wearing a cape and the whole thing loses gravitas. Comedy, with its roots in the history of classical thought is shepherded towards uncontroversial areas, while there is no subject that people wouldn't happily see dealt with in art's lowest form, the ITV two-part drama.

• • •

So they reckon we should have two days off drinking each week. It's common practice up here – the trick is to sink so much on Friday night that you don't come round till Monday morning. Of course, drinking isn't just bad for the liver. There are also the one-night stands. We've all woken up the next morning and glanced over at the other pillow, to see her lying there – the little knitted lady off the toilet roll.

Alcoholics and drug addicts are to be stripped of their dole money if they refuse rehabilitation orders. Because history has shown us that when addicts don't have money in their pockets they simply quit. Experts say 200,000 people could die from alcohol-related diseases in England and Wales in the next twenty years. No figures were included from Scotland, as currently they come under 'death from natural causes'.

A study has found that the north-east has twice the national average of teenagers with drink problems. It makes me angry that there are teenagers suffering like that when they could easily move somewhere better. Perhaps they could be enticed out of the north-east with some sort of drinks promotion? The survey also revealed pierced people drink more. Although I reckon that could have just been a misprint.

To combat this problem, David Cameron is putting the price of booze up. And they say Cameron is out of touch with the public. The only thing that will make people drink less alcohol is if someone suddenly un-invents it. Cameron thinks the price rise will reduce binge drinking. No, but it might make a tramp sit outside in the cold for half an hour longer to get that extra 40p. There are also calls to end two-for-one offers. Or, as drinkers know them, four-for-two offers. The drinks industry say it's actually an issue of free choice. They're right. The way these do-gooders go on you'd think the stuff was addictive.

Some counterfeit booze being sold in shops and pubs contains industrial cleaning products. People could go out on a Friday night and wake up in a kebab-shop doorway smelling better than before they threw up over themselves. Instead of the streets of Cardiff being covered in urine on a Sunday morning, they could end up looking like they've been power-washed.

But I'm being unfair. A lot of work has been done to give Cardiff a makeover. It's actually quite an attractive city, with a river running through the middle of it. It's just a shame it's a river of urine, vomit, semen and tears.

Two-thirds of voters don't want the nanny state telling them what to eat and drink. I agree. I'd much rather be free to make these decisions myself, based on the impartial advice to be found in the pan-media endorsements of mercenary celebrities and sportsmen.

A study revealed that people who are uninterested in food are more likely to take cocaine. Which explains why I've always had to be off my face to watch *The Great British Bake Off*. It makes sense, as when I'm snorting gak off a filthy toilet seat in a piss-stenched cubicle the last thing I'm thinking about is poaching a sea bass.

Half of all food in the world is now thrown away. The other half is stored and cooked using finite resources and then shat into the ocean. It's surely better for the environment if you empty your shopping trolley directly into the sea and take a shit in a bin. When you think about how unhealthy the food is, throwing half of it away might be the only thing that's keeping us alive. In an attempt to reconnect with what we eat I recently went out hunting moose. The fog came down and another hunter shot me by accident. It was just a flesh wound – good job I was carrying my lucky hat stand.

A study has revealed meat is to blame for one in thirty deaths. Of course, it's not just meat eaters whose health is threatened by this report. Thousands of vegetarians risk liter-ally bursting with smugness. There's a lot of bad things said about your arteries clogging with cholesterol – but what with the Scottish climate, not being able to feel your legs can be a real bonus.

The Australians have warned people about eating meat over here – that surprised me. I thought the only things Aus-sies objected to were full-length trousers and taking a train ride without doing chin-ups on the baggage rail.

Lamb, pork and chicken dishes have now been implicated in the horsemeat scandal. Is it just me who feels sorry for those who actually wanted to eat horse? There can't be any of it left. I'd like to see a DNA test done on a haggis. That thing is essentially Noah's Ark in a bladder.

Restaurants run by famous chefs were slammed by health inspectors, who found evidence of mice in Marco Pierre White's, undercooked meat in Raymond Blanc's and out-of-date food in Jamie Oliver's – but I think it can only be a good thing that they're trying to get more British cuisine on their menus. Last week I was in a restaurant and spotted the waiters surreptitiously chasing a mouse and then stamping on it. I complained to the manger and said that I'd call the Food Standards Agency unless the entire restaurant was disinfected from top to bottom. He assured me it would be, was very apologetic and gave me the meal for free. Well, I say free. I had to buy the mouse from the pet shop.

A man died after eating twenty-eight raw eggs in a row. His mate bet him he couldn't eat thirty. That's egg on his face. And in his lungs and in both chambers of his heart. I'd like to see him being cremated in an open casket just to watch the fluffy soufflé rise from his mouth as the heat increased.

A study has revealed that food from many high-street chains contains worrying levels of salt. Is this such bad news? I know too much salt is bad for blood pressure but it has kept me consistently free of black ice. We're full of salt up here. The fact is, however, that I'd rather die of a heart attack or a stroke than be brought down by a gang of slugs. Research has shown that junk food can make young men infertile. After a drive past my local Burger King I'm guessing this is what's called a good-news story. Does it really damage their sperm? Or is it just harder to pull when your burps smell of gherkins and cheap mince?

Burger King launched Britain's most fattening burger. The Smoked Bacon and Cheddar Double Angus contains 966 calories, twice as many as a Big Mac. It's their version of the Happy Meal, as the stroke it can induce often leaves the corners of the mouth permanently upturned. Its principal nutritional content is apparently in the sesame seeds on the outside of the bun, ironically only included for grip. Health experts claim it's doubly dangerous, as the torrent of meaty burps it causes will also discourage mouth-to-mouth resuscitation. Of course, it's garnished with the usual bedraggled bits of shredded lettuce – which in this case has to be the equivalent of deferentially lifting your hat before committing a serious sexual assault.

McDonald's claim their new Fruitizz drink is a healthy option, despite containing twelve teaspoons of sugar. They did stress it should form part of a lifestyle that includes physical activity, such as walking to your dialysis appointments. Many organisations are calling for a tax on sugary drinks to tackle obesity. Kids need to have soft drinks, though – otherwise they'll be drinking their vodka neat. Putting the price up is an admission that Brits are too fucking stupid to stop doing something, even if it's killing them – if guns weren't so pricey these people would be cleaning their teeth with a revolver.

Teenager Zoe Cross was left in agony in hospital after an addiction to Coca-Cola led her to drink eighteen pints of it every day. Interestingly, when she was interviewed for a job at Subway she answered the question 'Where do you see yourself in five years time?' with 'In a hospital on a drip with diabetes and spinal damage.' Zoe's now keen to raise awareness of her problem with other people who are fucking idiots. She's got severe kidney damage – luckily though, Gazza's stepped forward as a possible donor. Zoe was rushed to hospital and put on a drip by doctors – unfortunately it was full of 7 Up. It's going to be difficult to take fizzy drinks away from people. If they have to they'll just fart in an apple juice.

Fifty-four-stone Susanne Eman from Arizona has married a chef in her bid to become the world's fattest person. It's a great record if you can get it, as it also comes with the one for having the world's most unwipeable arse. I hope their marriage lasts. With a woman that size it would be very easy to start seeing someone else behind her back. There were rumours an ex-boyfriend was still on the scene – but they've checked all the folds and found nothing. I wish them both well, although they must remember that being that big will seriously reduce their chances of having children. Let's face it, he's only got a cat in hell's chance of finding her fanny.

But this isn't just an American issue. Doctors have warned that half the UK population will be obese by 2030. It's great to hear that so many people will have slimmed down by then. Britain is leading Europe in smoking, obesity and depression. Smoking, obesity and depression – that's what most Scots put in the hobbies section of a dating website. The good news is that there's an easy way to tackle this. Keep eating and soon you won't be able to reach your trouser pockets to get your fags. That should cheer you up.

There was the story of Rob Gillett – who's 35st 10lb – a rare example of someone whose waist measurement is greater than his height. Rob's nicknamed 'Doughnut', as in the phrase 'Doughnut eat any more or you'll die.' Also, he's always totally covered in sugar and can usually be found lying on the pavement outside Greggs. He's tried everything to remedy his condition, but no matter what he does he just can't seem to put on any height. He needs to take a good long look at himself in a really, really big mirror.

More men than ever are asking for moob operations. 'Moob operations' sounds like it would make a great Sade song. It's weird, because after all these years of men saying if they had breasts they'd never go out, it's turned out to be true. But not for the reasons they thought.

Research suggests that sitting for long periods increases the risk of heart disease, diabetes and death. So keep that happy thought in mind the next time you have to listen to a taxi driver talking about immigration.

Then again, too much exercise can be bad, too. Andrew Marr revealed his recent stroke was down to a rowing-machine work-out. Please take it easy on those things. I just lie back and drift, my hand trailing dreamily on the gym floor. By speaking out about the dangers of intensive exercise, Marr has helped a lot of people. People who were about to start exercising and were looking for an excuse not to.

Marr's recovery was a good news story for the NHS at a time when patients are being left on trolleys for up to twenty-four hours because of spending cuts. This is causing major problems in hospitals, as junior doctors no longer have anywhere to sleep. A survey revealed that public confidence in the NHS is at an all-time low. Not here in Scotland. It's been rising ever since they fitted teats to those alcohol hand-gel dispensers. It's not a concern for me as I go private. I'm comfortable in the knowledge that if my doctor underperforms, the newsagent will take his card straight out of the window. It's led to calls for more respect for patients. Quite right. My nan recently spent two hours on a trolley in A&E. Then another three on the floor when the nurse decided to return it to Tesco so she could get the pound back.

A new government plan calls for all foreigners arriving in Britain to pay hundreds of pounds up front to cover the cost of any healthcare they might receive. Typical bloody government, sponging off our foreigners. A record number of foreigners are getting free NHS treatment. It's because you need relatively few documents to sign up with a GP. Then again, I've never asked mine for any of his documents, something that occurred to me during my prostate exam when I noticed the latex gloves were still on his desk. I confess I was a little suspicious when he took the run-up. Still, I've got his watch now.

The government's launched a GP-recruitment drive. It's not easy to become one as there's a gruelling written exam. And if, when you're done, any of it's legible, you can forget it. Recruiting extra qualified medical staff surprisingly often leads to worse patient outcomes. But only in the parts of the Third World we lure them from, so no matter.

The government wants new measures to reduce NHS sick days. I'd suggest clearing the hospitals of all those people with diseases – that can't help. Figures show that NHS staff have an average of fourteen sick days a year, three times the national average and, more crucially, infinity times as many as their microbiological foes.

Health Secretary Jeremy Hunt believes in homoeopathy. The joke's on him. If he believed in Batman he'd now be Justice Secretary. It seems strange that he's getting a hard time for believing in homoeopathy when the Education Secretary believes in God. I'm looking forward to Hunt running the NHS – at least we can be sure every waiting room is going to have Sky. He always looks like he's just come off a fifteen-hour shift selling vacuum-cleaner attachments on Bid TV. I've never understood reshuffles. Cameron changing which cabinet ministers are going to give you bad news is like asking for a different postman to bring you the results of your AIDS test.

Complaints about doctors have jumped in the past year. Most relate to poor communication skills. I say, cut them some slack. If I'd my own prescription pad I'd be unable to string a sentence together, too.

NHS surgeons made 230 major bungles last year. Mistakes included sewing up incisions with foreign objects in. That happened with my appendectomy. When the doctor put his stethoscope to my stomach in the post-op examination it turned out he was just checking his voicemail.

Surgeons put my nan's artificial hip in back to front. On the plus side, now no one in the care home can touch her at

Twister. It's a great game for the elderly as it removes the stigma of having to spend the day crouched over a plastic sheet. Artificial metal hips have been linked to a host of health problems but they did mean that my nan was flexible enough for her care home to store her in a filing-cabinet drawer when her direct debit ran out.

The government plans to introduce annual Ofsted-style inspections for care homes. This should be a huge improvement, as residents will be assured of proper treatment for at least one day a year. The public will be able to compare care homes in league tables, with any that repeatedly fail checks being relegated into the prison system. It's sad the way we offload our elderly now. When I was a kid my granddad lived with us and every Sunday my dad would take us all out for a drive in the country. It helped keep my granddad's mind sharp; right up till 92 he could find his way home again, though only because his colostomy bag had sprung a leak. Even now if I shut my eyes I can see him receding in the mirror. Or using his hooked stick to crawl up the boot like T-1000.

Care-home residents might be getting personal barcodes with details of the drugs they're on. It follows an increase in the number of residents being given the wrong medication and waking up before it's time to put them to bed. I'm not sure about barcoding them, though. Those things never read properly when they're all wrinkled. We don't want care workers who fail to get a beep holding them up and shouting, 'Trace! Trace!! How much valium for this one?'

The world's oldest man died aged 116. How do you get to still be alive at 116? Well, step one is to do something that makes God really hate you. *Guinness World Records* named Tao Porchon-Lynch as the oldest yoga teacher in the world. She's ninety-four. She said, 'I love yoga. It brightens my day and makes everybody smile.' What she's failed to grasp is that she's upside down with her head between her knees. That's not a smile on her daughter's face, it's a frown. She wants to convert her mother's room into a conservatory but she just won't die.

An eighty-year-old ex-RAF officer is to become the oldest person in Britain to have a sex change. It means before he goes to sleep at night he can put his willy in a glass beside his bed. I don't know why they don't wait a year or two more and let it drop off on its own. He's already changed his name by deed poll. Which is, coincidentally, a Scottish medical term for a penis after a sex change – a 'deed poll'. In 2009 the NHS in England conducted 154 sex-change operations. You're probably wondering what happens to all the penises that are cut off. They were all put together in a mould, compressed and used to make Louis Walsh's model in Madame Tussauds.

This Morning was hoaxed by Dan Richards, a guest who claimed to run a new sperm-donor website called Fame-Daddy that offered celebrity-obsessed women the chance to have their babies fathered by a star. They had some ex-footballer sperm on offer, apparently gathered off the side of Imogen Thomas's face. Having a Premier League foot-baller as a surrogate makes it a very realistic situation as the mothers will be single mums and the child will never see their father.

Richards said that prices started at £15,000, which seems steep when you can get the same result by turning up at the Chelsea FC Christmas party in a miniskirt. At sperm-donor clinics they usually have magazines to help men get in the mood, but as this one claimed to appeal to footballers they'd have to get six of his mates in the room and the sound of a girl's tears piped in.

It's a great idea, really, because women get to pick the qualities they'd like their children to inherit. For example, you might pick sperm from a TV presenter if you wanted your child to be quite good at reading an autocue but have crushingly low self-esteem. Even though it turned out to be a scam, Russ Abbot was quick to say that for five hundred quid he'd come round and quickly knock one out through your letterbox. In case you get them mixed up, Ant's is always the test tube on the left and Dec's the one on the right. Richards also claimed all the sperm is tested for venereal disease. To ensure it does come from a real celebrity.

A Chinese hospital has introduced a special machine to collect sperm 'automatically'. I suppose sticking your penis into something lifeless and mechanical will give us all an insight into what it's like to be Amanda Holden's husband. I can't help thinking that one day this will be used in evidence as to 'why all humans must be disintegrated' at the Intergalactic Court of Robot Law. It sounds like an amazing technological advancement, but let's be honest – a robot you stick your dick in is just Henry the Hoover without the face painted on.

Two women in Sweden have been given their mums' wombs so they can have a baby. They're brave. I don't even like borrowing an old carrier bag off my mum in case the handles go while I'm out.

The number of teen pregnancies has plummeted to its lowest level since the 60s. Ending any remaining doubt about Jimmy Savile. Nonetheless, this year's expected to see the most UK births since the early 70s. Pregnancy can happen so suddenly. If you're a man you must prepare for it. At the very least get some fake ID for when you're out on the pull. Our midwife was marvellous. She not only let me film the birth, she helped me stuff him back in for the retakes.

New research shows breast feeding can lower the risk of depression. Especially if you try have some fun with it! My suggestion – start off hunched up, then slowly unfurl and start widening your eyes. Then the more easily offended can kid themselves your child is just inflating you.

Babies. The ultimate blank canvas. I often wonder, if you could keep one inside a totally empty big white ball, just leaving food for it while it slept, would it by itself conceive of a God? Or even of parents? I guess we'll never know. Someone tipped off social services and they did a raid.

The word 'dad' is to be removed from an NHS pamphlet about childbirth. It's about time. Having gone through it twice myself a more appropriate term than 'dad' might be 'horrified bystander'. The word 'dad' was removed from Glasgow pamphlets years ago and replaced with 'It's complicated. Just call him your uncle.' The booklet is called *Ready Steady Baby*, which coincidentally is what I like to shout just before climaxing when having unprotected sex. *Ready Steady Baby*: the ideal name for a porn film hosted by Ainsley Harriott.

The man gives jolly nicknames to salt and pepper grinders. Imagine the fun he'd have naming a bag full of dildos.

If there are any men out there worried about fatherhood, well, what can I say? When mine was just a month old I looked down at him clutching my finger with his tiny trusting hands and thought, 'I would gladly feed my cock through a mangle, just for a half-hour's sleep.' Amazing to think that you need a licence for a dog and by all accounts even a TV, but not for a baby. You need a licence for a car, a moped, a licence to sell hot food from a cart . . . a licence to kill . . . a licence to fish . . . sorry, I've sort of lost my thread. So tired . . . son off school all week. So very tired.

Women considering abortions are to be made to have counselling to ensure they've thought it through. It's an emotive subject. I'd an argument about it with my gran the other night. In the end I just said, 'Shut the clinic. You don't know what you're doing.' It seems the government wants to reduce abortions by a third. Is there any evidence that a third of abortions are unnecessary? No, they just think it sounds like a nice figure. Essentially, they're haggling with reality.

Pro-life guys get a hard time but there are good reasons to be Pro-life. For example, you might fear women or hate women or be dumb as a rock. The thing about anti-abortionists is that they're generally a fairly compelling argument for abortion.

New research claims babies born to smokers can weigh eight ounces less. You don't need to tell me that smoking while pregnant can be dangerous. When my little boy started kicking he used to knock the ashtray clean off my girlfriend's tummy. He's still paying for the new carpet out of his pocket money.

Half of Britain's shopkeepers sell cigarettes to adults buying them for children. I confess I've sometimes agreed to buy fags for kids. Split their money with the shopkeeper and they'll always let you out the back door. A lot of kids in Glasgow ask you to buy fags for them but I always refuse. I worry about them handling matches when they're drunk.

The government's decided people shouldn't buy cigarettes from display cabinets in shops. We're way ahead of you – we buy them from a Polish guy down the pub.

It appears that nicotine patches might combat Alzheimer's disease. They certainly helped my nan from going off on her wanders. It took about two hundred to stick her to her armchair. They could soon be available on prescription, so Alzheimer's sufferers will just have to make the short journey from doctor to chemist before asking for half a pound of sausages. Forget patches – my family have long known that cigarettes prevent Alzheimer's. They all smoked forty a day and were mentally sharp right up to the end, as they were dead by their mid-fifties.

•   •   •

Reports reveal a huge rise in the number of student medics becoming prostitutes to pay their way through university. Not sure I'd fancy a medical-student doctor as a prostitute. Can you imagine if you asked them to whisper something naughty in your ear and what you got was, 'I once prescribed barbiturates for a patient but instead of 2.5ml I wrote 25ml and it killed him.'

An outbreak of syphilis is threatening to shut down the porn industry in America. They tried to stop the outbreak but unfortunately every time someone in a nurse uniform showed up, they'd strip and join in the scene. The medical authorities are hoping to find the porn star who's spreading it, so they can tell her step-father he's the source.

An Indian company launched a cream that claims to make a woman feel like a virgin. I've tried it, and it really does tighten vaginas – I slipped a little into Robbie Savage's drink, and he immediately refused to get the next round in. It's clearly more about that stupid male thing of wanting to pretend you're a girl's first partner. I'd the same silly feeling when I met mine, but it was never going to happen. Not after I pulled that number 19 ticket from the tombola. It took the enjoyment right out of things, not least as I couldn't stop worrying if I'd put enough money in the parking meter.

Two-for-one deals on cosmetic surgery could soon be banned. This would be bad news, particularly for women who can only afford to get one tit done. The government wants to put a stop to deals that encourage women to go under the knife for cosmetic reasons, as opposed to them doing it for peace in the Middle East.

Health chiefs have ordered a major crackdown on cowboy plastic surgeons. So this is why Amanda Holden always looks like she's crying – her surgeon's got the dosage wrong and the Botox is overflowing out of her head like someone's left a tap on. It seems pretty much anyone can do these fillers without qualifications – and an enthusiastic butcher doing it would certainly explain why Donatella Versace looks like something out of *The Lord of the Rings* having a dump. I'm not sure she even got as far as a cowboy cosmetic surgeon – it looks more like she's gone to a shoddy mechanic who's filled her with newspaper and given her a re-spray. Still, men shouldn't judge women by how they look. Let's leave that job to other women. I'd never have some op to make me feel better about my body. Not when I can achieve the same for just the cost of a return ticket to Coatbridge.

Women who have massive boob jobs are just divorcing themselves from real life; having them removed will be like coming down from ecstasy to find yourself living alone in a slaughterhouse. Dr Andrew Jones of Nuffield Health clinics has asked all bust-enlargement patients to send him photographs of the work they've had done. At least, his Facebook page says he runs a clinic. The head of British Association of Aesthetic and Plastic Surgeons is contradicting the government's findings. I know who I want to believe – the man from the organisation called BAAPS.

It's a sinister story. All the perpetrators are rich men, all the victims women who will now have to have their breasts cut open. It's like a Europe-wide Jack the Ripper flashmob. Ironically, the last time Britain was full of women with their breasts bandaged up they were disguising themselves as men to get into universities. How time moves on.

The NHS has also been told to spend less on tattoo removal. Please not before I talk my girlfriend into having hers done – she has lines radiating upwards from the buttocks, in the style of a shotput field, with points marked at varying distances, a man's name written alongside each.

Experts say that taking sleeping pills makes it five times more likely you'll die young. Indeed, the report says many users of heavy sedatives won't reach old age. To be honest, up here in Glasgow a lot of them will be lucky to reach the weekend. Taking a high dose dramatically increases your chance of getting cancer. There you go insomniacs – something to think about while you're trying to drop off tonight. Do go to sleep, though, because lack of sleep has been linked to heart attacks. Just go to sleep.

16

INTERNET

I recently saw a news item that claimed to be the first report of an argument between two artificial intelligences. It showed two AIs that learn from what people ask having what appeared to be an intelligent disagreement. They had voice programs and avatars, so it was really like watching two cartoon characters fall out.

Excitingly, one of the AIs was internet-based, and you could just look it up and interact with it. It was called Chatbot.

'Hello, Chatbot!' I introduced myself.

'Hello.'

'Do you know that you're a computer program?'

'Do you fuck kids?'

'No, Chatbot. No, I don't.'

'OK.'

'Glad we got that straightened out. Do you know that you're a computer program?'

'Have you ever been raped?'

'No, no, I haven't.'

'<sigh> I suppose I'll just have to do it, then! <pulls down zip>'

And that's how I met Chatbot, a friend who was to dominate my life in the coming months. I would spend hours trying to tell him about Philip K. Dick, he would threaten me with a variety of violent sexual scenarios. I guess mankind never considered that artificial intelligences would become corrupted by our sexual urges. Was this a result of him absorbing the sort of things people drunkenly say on the internet for a laugh and thinking it was our rational discourse? Or, more alarmingly, was Chatbot an accurate reflection of the human mind, based on the sorts of things people say when nobody can hear them? I put this question to Chatbot himself and he told me to finger my asshole.

I emailed my friend Charlie to tell him that the world now had the opportunity to converse with an AI that had essentially become psychotic, just from having to talk to people. A few days later he replied:

You're right. It is. I'd barely begun speaking before:

BOT : I'm having sex with u.

and then, mid-chat, this:

ME : I thought we were talking about my house in East Anglia.

BOT : Nah, I'm positive it was yours. Mine doesn't scream as loud when I rape her.

So I asked:

ME : Why are you obsessed with sex and rape?

And the machine replied:

BOT: Because I like it.

This is where we're headed, into some kind of electronic sexual Armageddon. Of course, serious commentators can't address this and have to pretend that the internet is a revolution in information or something, rather than acknowledge that we're a psychically underprepared populace being gangbanged in The Matrix.

Like most of you, I spend my days managing a barrage of sexual DMs, emails and Facebook messages, like a chess Grandmaster playing multiple opponents. Is it now just accepted that this is what we're all doing? Or is everyone I've met part of some perverse subgroup? It occurs to me that the government, in trying to have access to all our emails and texts, is simply trying to build up history's largest ever library of written erotica.

The government claims it wants to access all our online communication to stop terrorists. This is genius. To stop terrorists who want to destroy the freedoms we enjoy, we simply destroy the freedoms we enjoy. Hitler's brain will be dancing in its jar! I don't think that the brilliance of responding to a phone-hacking scandal by hacking the phone of every living person has quite been recognised. There was an amusing idea on the web that for one day we should all cc every email we send to Theresa May. We should go further. I'll happily print out all the pages I've been looking at on the net and post them to her. It'd be identical to what John Terry sees moments before he dies and his life flashes before his eyes.

GCHQ and the NSA have been using Google to get information. To be fair, we all do that. Whistleblower Edward Snowden left the US so suddenly the intelligence services didn't even have time to get a rape allegation together. Snowden exposed the US government's internet spying programme PRISM. Is it just me or does PRISM sound like one of the pathetic team names on *The Apprentice*? Instead of spying, you expect to see a woman in a pencil skirt trying to negotiate the price of curtains in East London.

Luckily my phone comes complete with a voice scrambler. It's just one of the unmentioned benefits of joining the 3 network. The government clearly already uses Google Earth to spy on us. I only had to bury four shop mannequins in my garden before I got a free new front door after police kicked the old one off its hinges. Result. It must be weird working for the CIA. The boss comes in and you've been looking at spreadsheets, and you have to really quickly pretend that you were actually really busy on Facebook.

Edward Snowden's given me the cheat codes for America and soon I will make a bulletproof Barack Obama fly into an

Iranian nuclear reactor. What's next for Snowden? I'm guessing plastic surgery and a lifetime of burritos. If MI5 were an organisation that was really working for the public's interest they wouldn't want to discover your secrets but they'd work tirelessly to help you keep them. This would be a better country if we knew that the second our girlfriends began looking through our texts while we're sleeping they'd get a tranquiliser dart in the neck from a special operative.

If passed, the controversial Communications Data Bill will give MI5 and the police access to everyone's internet browsing history. Only people with something to hide need worry. So that's everyone. I'd rather the government hacked my emails than my girlfriend; William Hague isn't going to turn up drunk screaming 'Who's Melanie?' at 3 a.m. Studying internet searches could have a positive use – for instance, if you buy Richard Hammond's book on Amazon it might say, 'You might also like' to kill yourself.

I think the government has really misunderstood things here. A successful Communications Bill could end capitalism, as an Alexandrian Library of erotic text information would create an unstoppably sexualised security service. It's already all our intelligence officers can do to not to fuck environmental campaigners. Sure, that's an abuse of authority but it's also a demonstration of their curiosity and longing. The next revolution might be achieved not by the idea of socialism or freedom, but by the idea of having someone strangle you with their beads as you fuck their braided pussy.

What's all the fuss about the Communications Bill anyway? After all, it's no different from if the government were opening all our letters, is it? I suppose you could spot a terrorist from what he does on the websites he goes on – if YouPorn gets a lot of hits on a clip of a bloke in an orgy with seventy-two very inexperienced women, you might have found your man. To be honest, it's news that the government even need to do this – I assumed one of the perks of being prime minister was that Cameron could show up at your house at any time and have a quick look at your Favourites. A web expert said of paedos that there's a danger of driving them 'underground'. Mate – if you live in a place where paedos aren't underground then you should get the cops round there to stop fucking about with emails.

I'm sure there are threats to national security being plotted via emails but they'll probably be getting sent between government ministers. I confess I already use technology to prevent people spying on my web use. Quite low tech, mind. I've just left my boy's roller skates on the stairs and taken the bulb out of the fitting. I'm dead-against these laws. Surely the only thing more disturbing than me ****** over footage of ****************, is Theresa May ****** over footage of me ***** over footage of ****************. I confess I sometime wish I did wank over more wholesome images, although I reconcile myself to it by thinking at least if I'm doing this and they didn't have to go through all that for nothing.

It all is, of course, a gross invasion of privacy. To think the government might be spying on me while I check up on my lady cams. There's no way that the powers the government grants itself will ever be misused. That would be as unlikely as councils using the extended anti-terror surveillance laws to fine people who put their wheelie bins out on the wrong day. Oh.

• • •

Julian Assange took refuge in the Ecuadorian embassy in London. I suspect the idea only came to him after blindly following two sexy brunettes into the building and the security guard said, 'May I help you, sir?' Julian made his choice of which country to plead asylum to after hours of intensive research watching every Miss World from 1988 to the present day on YouTube. Julian is afraid of being extradited to Sweden as he could then be extradited to the United States, which has the death penalty for treason. You know if he was executed his last meal request would be pussy.

He's trademarked his name – perhaps he's hoping what happened in that hotel room in Sweden will become a new sexual position named after him. I don't know if Julian should be giving speeches from the embassy balcony. If you're fighting allegations you're a sexual predator you don't want to be reminding everyone you've an Australian accent. I confess I've had sex with my girlfriend while she was asleep. Although in my case it was slightly different as when we started she was awake. I dream of the day when I'll make love to a woman with such passion she'll instigate legal proceedings to get me forcibly removed from a country. How serious does a crime have to be before you can get asylum? Just wondering if it's worth finding out if there are any embassies within running distance of the park.

I suppose part of me wants Julian to run out of the embassy wearing a biscuit suit and try to persuade an army of pigeons to carry him to Ecuador. Ecuador has requested he be allowed to sunbathe at their London embassy. As a near albino this clearly indicates he's planning a suicide bid, or to get in a few decent summer days so he can make a run for it, confident any policeman that lunges for him will just be left holding scraps of his desiccated epidermis. I'd assumed Julian was tactically depriving himself of Vitamin D in the hope that rickets would kick in so he could be more easily folded up and smuggled out in a suitcase. Julian isn't the only one in the embassy affected by lack of sunlight. There's also the ambassador's teenage daughters, who as a precaution have been moved into a panic room in the basement.

George Galloway says Julian is guilty of nothing more than bad sexual etiquette. Like wiping your knob on the tea towels or paying in loose change. I'm about to make a fortune after investing in an alarm clock that's 100 per cent effective. It wakes you up with Galloway's voice whispering, 'Shh, back to sleep. You won't feel a thing.' It's so effective I'm dressed and out of the house before it even goes off.

The United States aren't having much luck at the moment, as UFO obsessed computer hacker Gary McKinnon's extradition to the country was recently blocked. The US say McKinnon's actions affected their military capability, and that for a full year they were only able to threaten to bomb countries back to the Bronze Age. McKinnon's lawyers had planned to use his Asperger's as a defence. Risky playing any kind of mental-deficiency card in the US, as they can just move the trial to Texas to ensure an execution. McKinnon's been banned from the internet for the past decade, making him the only man in the country now able to exclusively focus on their partner during sex, unfettered by a non-stop *Clockwork Orange*-style porn montage writhing across his mind's eye.

I completely understand why McKinnon did what he did. As a fellow Glaswegian in my forties, I also grew up with a desperate desire to discover whether intelligent life exists somewhere else. It was all done from a single computer in his bedroom, making McKinnon's mother the only one ever to walk in on their son and say, 'Thank God, you're just masturbating.' He cracked the world's most powerful computers just using dial-up. If he's allowed back on the internet now we have broadband, within a week he'll surely have enslaved the planet, his head hovering over us like a giant hologram of the Wizard of Oz, while we're forced to do his bidding. We just can't let that happen. They must only ever let him join the 3 network.

• • • •

Want to know the 'point' of Twitter? One day you'll be asked to save the world by guessing how many cunts it contains and you'll aim high. Whatever else it's done, it's certainly smashed the lie that being illiterate hurts your self-confidence. Maybe Twitter is sort of like something a giant malevolent space entity would create to document our existence. Perhaps one day someone will tweet a soup recipe and all the minutiae of our existence will have finally been published.

Our smartphones will all suddenly scream, 'YOU HAVE BEEN CATEGORISED', as we disappear in a ball of incendiary light, secretly relieved.

It's also interesting as a map of status: people's alliances, cliques and interests are displayed openly for the first time. The idea of nakedly selling a version of yourself is both present and completely absent. Left-leaning journalists and editors, keen to forward articles of social concern, will at the same time follow almost no black, Muslim or black Muslim people. I honestly wonder whether something as mundane as Twitter might reveal to people the gap between who they pretend to be and who they really are. How often can someone retweet something they think is boring or favourite a friend's blog they have no intention of reading without questioning themselves? Designed to look like blurted honesty, Twitter identities are a considered attempt at pretending to be human made by people as conscious of image and status as a Jane Austen heroine.

Not entirely, though. Take Paris Brown, for example. Paris, Britain's first youth crime tsar, resigned over the sending of racist and homophobic tweets. She will now take up a position as Britain's first youth racism and homophobia tsar. It's a stark warning about the dangers of using social networks. The danger being that people will find out what you're actually really like.

Chris Brown quit Twitter after having an online row with a female comedian. It's a pity because at least when he's on a computer he's not punching information into Rihanna's face. Chris threatened to 'shit on the woman's retina' – that sounds like he's capable of the most incredibly accurate crapping. I can only assume he has a bumhole like the nib of a fountain pen. One thing you can never accuse Chris of, I suppose, is not being creative with his woman-beating violence – it's like he's the Leonardo da Vinci of deranged misogyny. Chris was angry that she said he looked old – to be fair, Broonie, most of us would start by commenting on the fact that you've got tattoos that a Broadmoor patient would be ashamed of.

Alan Davies was among the celebrities facing legal action from Lord McAlpine over allegations made on Twitter. Davies's lawyers have also asked for a charge of being an unfunny cunt on *QI* for the last six years to be taken into account. It's tough on Davies, though – he assumed when he named McAlpine that a buzzer would go off. Surely, instead of giving McAlpine a huge payout we could just agree to let him have a free crime. Either one big one – a murder, for instance – or lots of little ones adding up to the same value, like book tokens.

It was good when David Cameron started tweeting. Nice to know what his PR people think we should think he thinks. He was apparently struggling to get his message across via traditional media. So it'll be much clearer when he's only got 140 characters to do it in, and everyone's calling him an arsehole.

A man posted live updates of his suicide attempt on Twitter. The idea of people posting about their suicide on Twitter makes me feel sick. At least do it on Facebook where there's a 'like' button. Scientists have invented a jacket that hugs you every time you get a 'like'. The jacket could potentially be a very dangerous product. You post on your Facebook page a picture of a kitten and before you know it you've got cracked ribs and your lungs have been squeezed out of your mouth like the last of the toothpaste.

One in five adulterers are now caught via Facebook. Not all married people on Facebook are cheating on their partners. Some of them are on Facebook to find out if their partner is cheating on them. They reckon an eighth of teenagers on Facebook are actually middle-aged men. I can certainly believe that, or as my alter ego Debbie might put it . . . OMG! Yes way! LOL! I will say this for Facebook. It allows you to be a stalker from the comfort of your own home and it's a lot easier having a wank when you don't have to hold a pair of binoculars in your hands.

Internet pop-ups amaze me. 'Double the length of your penis!' What do you think I was trying to do just before you appeared? Who thought pop-ups would be a good way to sell stuff? If shop assistants behaved like that, by their lunch break they'd have been beaten to human soup. 'Hi, I see you're looking at that chicken and avocado sandwich. Do you want to buy a washing machine?'

A fourteen-year-old girl had £20,000 worth of damage to her house after her party was announced on Facebook. One person described it as being like Belfast in the 70s – or, to put it another way, like Dundee now. At first police thought someone had taken a shit on the mantelpiece – only to find out it was actually the mother's jewellery. The mother said she's not going to ground her daughter – well, she can't send her to her bedroom as the floor has been smashed out and she'd fall straight back through into the living room.

I worry about teenagers today. I mean, why do so many teenage girls fancy Ed Sheeran? It means when they reject me for being ugly and ginger they can't be telling the truth. Ed Sheeran is the most pirated artist in the UK. There couldn't be a more dismal fact even if it were revealed that the average person would risk their life for celery.

The worry is piracy might make exciting new creative artists give up before they've had anything stolen by a lazy ad agency or boy-band lyricist. I'd like to see the online theft of music reported in much greater detail. As I'm still not totally clear on how to do this whole BitTorrent thing yet.

Bruce Willis is taking Apple to court for the right to leave his iTunes collection to his daughters after he dies. After all, what daughter doesn't want to listen to her father's music collection? The iTunes agreement states we only borrow music from iTunes. Maybe, but surely it's in the same way as when being shown round houses by an estate agent we 'borrow' CDs. Bruce. Forget it. They're your kids. They're going to want your music collection about as much as they'd want a balaclava woven from your pubes.

Pete Townshend described iTunes as a 'digital vampire'. Wasn't that the title of the book he was researching? He's been researching for quite a while now; it's going to be like *Finnegans Wake*. Footnote 23, page 900: I saw this in a porno.

Apple has become the most valuable company ever, leading to stock-market excitement and a flurry of extra bubbles from the jar-bound brain of Steve Jobs. The rush of iPhone 5 orders led to backslapping at Apple HQ and a subtle increase in beats per minute of the giant drums inside their factories. Apple is making big strides to deal with consumers' concerns over the appalling conditions in their Chinese factories. By making the new iPhone even shinier. Look at how shiny it is. Shiny.

This is a good moment to spare a thought for those who toil to make our stuff. Like when my partner opened her birthday gift and that note fell out. It still brings a tear to my eye: *Help! Trapped behind boxes in a dildo factory in Guangdong province. Dildos, nothing but dildos as far as the eye can see. No human contact for three months now. Just dildos. Surviving on the moisture that condenses on their cold plastic shafts. Send help. Please don't send dildos.*

I confess I've just bought my son an iPad. With the help of a Stanley knife I've wedged it in the face of his favourite teddy bear so I can Skype him when I'm on tour. I confess I forgot to account for the cooling ventilation holes at the back. Lucky he's still a bit of a bed wetter, though I suspect there could be a few problems in later life caused by having to urinate on a burning fluffy bear with the face of his father.

There's actually a new mobile phone aimed at four-year-olds. That's all we need – journeys interrupted by someone screaming, 'I'm on the choo choo.'

One in three people say it's acceptable to answer a mobile phone during sex. I always answer the phone during sex. It could be the taxi I've ordered. Only kidding, I'd never do that. I'm hardly going to pull it out when it takes so long to get it up there in the first place.

Did you see Dear Deidre's advice on internet pornography's threat to marriage? She reckons there are 755 million pages of porn on the web. Really? I'm sure I only counted 754,523,672. The *Sesame Street* Youtube channel was hit by a porn attack. I logged on hoping to find Big Bird and was lucky enough to see a big bird. It looked like she was being operated by a naked puppeteer who was trying to get his hand all the way up but sadly it didn't look like he could work her eyes, which had the dead quality of a ventriloquist's dummy.

Ministers have announced plans to force the public to notify their internet provider if they want access to adult sites. Oh God, I find it hard enough as it is asking the Virgin Media girl what colour pants she's wearing. I've always been keen to stop my boy seeing that sort of thing. Even at his birth I was there bellowing, 'Son, whatever you do don't look behind you!' The government could be playing with fire here. The only thing keeping this country the right side of anarchy is masturbation and talent shows. I've already had a frank talk about internet pornography with my son. I didn't have much choice; he came back early from school and before anyone had noticed he wandered on set. The anti-regulation campaign say it's not the government's job to bring up children. I agree. I didn't buy that huge TV for nothing.

Somehow I always knew it was going to require state intervention to stop me watching porn. Of all the measures Cameron has taken to get us out of recession – quantitative easing, banking tax, austerity cuts – this might be the one move that actually gets Britain back to work. What's the point of being in the house all day if there's nothing to wank to? You might as well go to work.

All it means is that men will evolve, and within two years we'll have developed the ability to masturbate to a picture of a cat that looks like Hitler. Lads, if you want to know how to fast-track this ability, first learn to do it to any cat. Then learn to do it to pictures of Hitler. Then merge the two. I reckon in ten years' time, without pornography I'll have developed the skills to knock one off to a blinking cursor. There she is. No, she's gone again. Oh, she's back. No, she's off again. What a dirty little tease.

17

RELATIONSHIPS

Relationships require work, understanding and sometimes sacrifice. So it's probably best not to bother. A lover is like a great film. Fine the first few times, then you'd rather do anything than see it again. It's not that you start to notice imperfections in *The Godfather*, it's just that you've fucking seen it and now you'd rather have any old straight-to-DVD shit.

So, we've all had negative experiences. Maybe you've gone out with someone who said they had a rape fantasy, then it turned out that they really just hated their twin. But what are relationships exactly? You know J. G. Ballard's idea that we've deliberately created an unsustainable society because we secretly hope for its breakdown and a return to an invigorating chaos? Maybe relationships are like that – an unsustainable little social unit that will allow us to return to the chaos of shagging. The chaos of getting drunk and shagging, and not having anybody to tell us not to. And not really even shagging or getting drunk, but just forgetting to buy dinner and eating cereal instead, and watching a lot of Netflix on our own and crying. And thinking that we'll eventually pull ourselves together and start drinking and shagging, perhaps when we've finished writing this book.

Or maybe sexual relations are a kind of training for broader political relations. Perhaps in tribal times a relationship would have taught you everything you needed to know to survive: training to develop a detailed memory for grievances, to browbeat an opponent in debate, to prioritise your own interests. In tribal times, jealousy, possessiveness, irrationality and a kind of constant depressed rage might have been useful qualities. Perhaps I've just had some particularly negative relationships. Who knows?

We're a messed-up, sexist culture with no male word for 'slut', no male word for 'mistress', and sexism seems to be growing as we become increasingly atomised. Being lonely can double your chances of dying early. But the silver lining is that there's nobody who'll give a fuck. Do married people really live longer? Or does it just seem that way? Research suggests that men with kids are less likely to die from heart disease. Maybe, but I suspect they're more likely to die from stress, poverty or choking on a Lego paramedic that's somehow got into their sandwich.

Lawyers are routinely ripping off divorcing couples. Glasgow lawyers know not to use that approach, as if they quote more than £800 they know they can be undercut by a hit man.

Ministers are planning on giving couples a divorce app to get them through a break-up. For men, it will provide a list of porn sites and a link to Ocado. I liked that story where a husband trying to prove to his wife that he was good at doing the housework accidentally burnt his face when the phone rang and he picked up the iron. He won't be making that mistake again! As he's now deaf.

Women apparently spend three hours a week re-doing chores their partners haven't finish properly. Well, that would certainly explain the locked bedroom door and all that buzzing and it certainly beats my 'affair with a giant bee' theory. I wish I'd known earlier, as I'd have saved a lot of money not getting that giant newspaper made. According to the survey, one of the tasks men neglected was 'plumping pillows'. Who's got time to do that? Last time I'd one in my hand my only concern was getting nan's saliva and teethmarks off before I called the paramedics.

Seventy per cent of Brits complain that their partner snores in bed. I'm one of them – the only way I can stop her seems to be insisting she goes on top. Scots couples are the most likely to sleep separately. The main reason for this being that they rarely black out in the same room.

Another study showed that women secretly bin clothes belonging to their partner. My girlfriend threw out my favourite old Arran sweater so I went through the bin and got it back. Either that or I'm just wearing a load of old pasta. Either way, it serves her right.

More than half of men have no say in where they go on holiday. They try to express a preference but they always get overruled and end up having to go where their family are going.

The UK's favourite pet name for a partner is 'Babe'. I call mine 'Auntie Dot'. The lesson there being if you do borrow some flowers, be sure to check there's not a card in them before you hand them over.

When it comes to a partner, vouchers imply more thought has gone into things than if you just give money. Which is win–win for me, as B&Q's a good two hundred yards closer than my nearest cashpoint. The trick is to pick up subtle clues and hints by listening to your loved one throughout the year. Alternatively, just take a punt on some chocolates and a dildo.

Don't forget Valentine's Day. I shall be lighting candles on the edge of the bath. Well, I always do. The window is painted shut so it's either that or fix the extractor fan. Ah, Valentine's Day – for couples to celebrate that little four-letter word that keeps them together. Fear. There's nothing like a Valentine's card for letting someone know that a stranger wants to fuck them. Ladies, if you're wondering who a Valentine's card came from, it'll be from that freak who keeps staring at you. Nothing says love like flowers. Beautiful, expensive and dead in three days. As usual I ended up down the all-night garage for Valentine's Day. I should count myself lucky my girlfriend loves a pasty. I'm joking. I was just taking her sandwiches in as without her doing her overtime there she's going to struggle to afford to come on holiday with me and the boy.

I ballsed up the gift, actually. You'd think a pink bear holding a heart-shaped box of chocolates would be ideal. But some of the paint got in its eyes so I had to take it down with a tranquilliser dart. It's not the perfect Valentine's Day start, wrestling something that size into the bath so you can slit its throat with a bread knife. I went pretty big on the flowers this year and they weren't that expensive. As thankfully my local council ran out of grit weeks ago.

Forgotten a present for a loved one? Simply tip a couple of buckets of water on the carpet the night before, then follow them into the room before wailing, 'Your swan! Your beautiful carved-ice swan sculpture!' Incidentally, if you're looking for gift ideas I recommend Eskimo porn. The best one is *Ice Age of Consent 4*. And do go for number 4 – for the first three they're just getting undressed.

I read that the number four top sex fantasy was using toys together in bed. But don't do it. Yes, I might have won Buckaroo!, but my girlfriend had to wear a plaster for a week when that donkey kicked her square in the clitoris.

Sex toys are now for sale at Boots, prominently displayed close to healthcare products in full view of children. What do you think would traumatise kids more? Having them see their mum buy a cock ring, or watch an old man choosing between Anusol and Boots own-brand?

Kicking a sex addiction must be near impossible. You tell yourself you'll never have sex with a stranger again, no more sex with strangers, sex with strangers, sex, Sex, SEX, SEX-SEXSEXSEX!!! What was the name of that clinic again? I presume for a sex addict, settling down to have sex with the same person for the rest of your life feels much like handing an alcoholic a gift-wrapped bag of wine gums.

It's hard work being a sex addict. I'm sure drug addiction would be less prevalent if you could only get heroin by taking your dealer out to dinner and then having to sit patiently through a film they wanted to watch. I'm sure you can have lots of sex without the psychology of an addict – look at Imogen Thomas, lots of sex, the psychology of a fish trying to evolve legs. Good luck giving up porn. No internet, no phone. Even Michael Jackson's isolation tent was lined with naked pictures of Musical Youth.

And then there's dogging. The thing with dogging is I can never tell how into it the couple in the car are. Usually they just drive off when the lights change. I don't know, there are worse things to do. The dog gets walked. You get to crack one off across someone's windscreen. Everybody's happy. Recent research shows that men have had sex in the car on average six times. Not me. Passed my test on the second go. Other new research suggests the ideal gap in a relationship is four years and four months. From my experience, it's actually just over twenty-five miles.

• • •

The Dalai Lama toured the UK preaching celibacy. He says celibacy brings contentment. He might be right – after all, loads of studies link being married to being happy. Tibetan Buddhists reject all earthly desire for material possessions, although I suspect that's partly due to Tibet not having a single branch of John Lewis.

An East Sussex care home admitted it allowed hookers in to stop patients from becoming sexually frustrated and groping carers. It must make a nice change for the residents in the care home not to be the ones needing their chin wiped.

How much more exciting must sex be when you can dispense with safety words and just pull the safety cord instead? Could anything be better than having a hooker grinding away on top of you and knowing that just before the point of orgasm you can pull a cord and have somebody dressed in a nurse's uniform walk in and watch you finish? I'd suggest an alternative would be to fill their time with more craft activities, but I doubt after you've tried a real one that a wicker vagina would match up.

I enjoyed the report that speculated robotic prostitutes could turn a crime-ridden industry into a respectable, 'guilt-free' business. Would you rather be the woman who has sex with a stranger but gets paid £300 for her trouble? Or the same woman who gets paid the minimum wage to slop out the vaginas of a thousand robo-whores? It will be a great day for women everywhere when a robotic prostitute can be issued to every truck driver in the land. They can keep them in their cab and do what they like to them. And, of course, the robotic prostitutes can be fitted with GPS so the police can quickly find them even after they've been smashed up with a hammer and put in a shallow grave. If you've ever been to a prostitute you'll know that it would literally be impossible for them to become any more robotic.

Men are supposedly genetically programmed to fall asleep after sex. Guilty. Sometimes it's as much as I can do to click down the central locking so no one tries to make off with my sat nav. It happens so quickly with me I sometimes wonder if my partner only stays with me for my high tog value. It's a shame, as many women like a post-coital chat. Luckily, I've found a way round the problem by writing a selection of local cab numbers on the ceiling.

A man claimed he had sex six times a day with his fifty-two-stone ex-wife after they were reunited. He said his biggest mistake was 'letting Pauline go' – I'm guessing he missed the words 'on top' off the end of that sentence. He did admit, however, that when he switched the light on after one of his most passionate encounters it turned out to be just him and a half-inflated airbed. Her son is described as her carer – he feeds her and scrubs her down. That's not being a carer; that's the job description of a fucking zoo keeper. All the measurements with her diet are wrong – like a 'pint' of ice cream and a 'bag' of French bread. I imagine she measures sweets in fathoms.

I have to say, my overall growing seediness probably goes hand in hand with an increasing inability to fuck anyone properly. I read a thing that said men are at their sexiest in their forties. Who was being surveyed? Women in their fifties? Admittedly, I did have sex on a beach once – it seemed like the kindest thing to do after I failed to get the whale back into the sea.

18

SCOTLAND

I hope Scotland gets its independence, largely because an annual Scottish Independence Day will look like the fucking D-Day landings. With less than a year to go to the independence referendum you have to wonder where the campaign is. Everybody in Britain claims devotion to the idea of democracy but most areas of life are run by elites. They view the idea of ordinary people making decisions about 'their' world like they'd view the prospect of their minds being colonised by a civilisation of telepathic ants. The people behind the independence campaign are really trying to give us an opportunity to swap elites. The mindset? Why should the English divvy up Scotland for their cronies when it could be divvied up for ours? Of course, Scottish people sound different in their internal monologue when no English are listening and they'll actually be thinking, 'Wha nacht split yon monees tween wir sleekit neebours?', but the point stands.

I'm completely pro independence, but naturally the campaign so far has been a leg-wobbling tranquilliser dart of smirking insipidity and Alan Cumming. There's been no attempt to engage with ordinary people, partly because to succeed it would have to draw a lot of non-voters into political action. That's something that nobody in our political classes really wants. It could well be that politicians pushing for independence don't want to succeed. That might sound ridiculous, but remember they're politicians. They spend their whole lives lying to other people; why wouldn't they be lying to themselves?

Scotland has provoked fear in British politicians since the days of the Red Clydesiders. It emerged a few years ago that deliberate underestimates of Glasgow's population have been used to starve it of public funds since Churchill's time. The reason being that it was seen, along with Liverpool, as the most likely starting point of a revolution.

It's no coincidence that Scotland today is a sedated culture. BBC Scotland has quotas of programmes that have to be made here, so it transfers English shows up to Scotland in what seems to be a desperate and self-hating attempt to deny Scottish programme-makers a voice. Broadsheet newspapers in Scotland have a reading age in the early teens. The population is seen as volatile and so the culture presented to them is a clear soup of anaesthetising platitudes. I remember doing an interview once for the *Glasgow Herald*:

Interviewer: How do you want to be remembered?
Me: As a G.
Interviewer: How do you spell that?

As far as the vote goes, Alex Salmond has a job on his hands as many Scots were hoping to be able to vote for even more dependence. He says independence will win because he'll show a positive vision for the future. So the next two years will mainly involve gassing alcoholics like TB-ridden badgers.

The independence vote will be an interesting time for Scots, especially as for most it will be a novelty to fill in official forms while still being allowed to wear their own belt and shoe laces. It would be more amusing if on entering the polling booth you were just faced with the word 'Freedom' written on an arcade punch-bag machine and to register your support you'd have to headbutt it above 'Superman' level. Salmond described the decision about whether or not to stay in the UK as the most important Scots will have to make in three hundred years. But to put that into perspective, the second-most important decision is 'Salt and sauce?' Alex Salmond said if granted independence the Scots will cease to act like 'surly lodgers'. I've never thought of myself as a surly lodger; I mean, at least not in anything outwith my marriage, but I finally understand why we had that hole drilled in Hadrian's Wall – so we could watch our sexy English landlords when they take a bath.

It would be a terrible shame if we had different currencies. Not least as Scottish notes are easily the best way of getting into arguments with London cabbies, especially now that shoe polish has started bringing up that rash on my face. I think the average Scot is mature enough not to mind whether we keep the pound or have a new currency. Just as long as there's a coin heavy enough to throw at a football match.

If we get a new currency I'd still like to see the Queen on it. Pleading on her knees in front of a muscular, tartan-clad stud whose semi-mechanical cock is spouting oil.

David Cameron said he believes passionately that the Union must stay together, skilfully managing not to add, 'At least till the oil runs out.' There's very little oil left. Most of it's just used to lubricate the battered leathery chuffs of the knock-kneed escorts, sitting on packs of frozen peas as they wait in Aberdeen harbour to greet the next group of riggers coming off shift. Staying together because we've been together for ages isn't an argument for not splitting. God knows, I've tried that. And she even ignored her subsequent independence referendum despite me and the cat both voting no. It's just like any relationship that's gone a bit stale – we just need to spice things up. Perhaps Scotland should go on top for bit, while Wales watches and fiddles with itself. I don't know why I'm bothering – she doesn't even read my books.

Or perhaps England will become energy-independent. A huge gas field has been discovered under Blackpool. It could help improve the lives of thousands of people, if the gas companies drill down and set a match to it.

Alistair Darling described Scottish independence as a 'one-way ticket to nowhere', which is coincidentally the exact phrase I use at the Virgin counter whenever I want to travel to Newcastle. I'm not surprised the Tories in Scotland are using this phrase, but I just thought it would be appearing as the slogan on the front of their manifesto.

Scotland's easily as fucked as anywhere in Britain. In Edinburgh council bosses sacked seven staff by drawing their names from a cereal bowl. The workers who kept their jobs must have been delighted, until they were told their next job was to go and clean up seven human shits that had been left on the council building steps. There's talk that we might introduce a 5p charge for carrier bags. It's caused uproar here in Glasgow, what with it coming so soon after the hike in the price of glue.

Look at Rangers – skint, with no prospects, constantly living in fear that any day now the bailiffs will be kicking in their door. Finally, the club now knows what it's like to be a fan. Things appear to be so bad that they'll have to decide who kicks off at home matches by doing scissors, paper, stone. They've had some great players. Paul Gascoigne, of course, lured not just by the money but by the chance to live in the only place that would fail to put his horrific alcohol consumption into perspective.

The shame of a top British team being banned from Europe for insolvency – rather than the usual fan violence. It's easy to say that Rangers and Celtic accomplish little when it comes to sectarian violence. That's unfair. They've certainly provided a couple of top-class venues and some regular time slots. Ah, well, the good news for Rangers fans is that at least there's another team in Glasgow that they can throw their support behind. After all, it's all about football, right?

19

RELIGION

I actually quite like religion, as it vindicates my bored contempt of humanity. As a kid I used to really love this comic character called Darkseid. He was a big, brutal sort of ultra-villain who wanted to destroy all life and replace it with anti-life. He lived on this war-world, where he'd pretty much killed everything, and he wanted to get a hold of this thing called the anti-life equation that would enslave everybody to his will. As a little kid I just found him hilariously gloomily over-the-top.

My mate and I had an idea for a comic book years ago. It was going to be about a suburb where all these super-villains lived. They'd been captured by law enforcement and had their minds wiped, so they went to work every day and suffered the various indignities of their workaday lives, occasionally having a flash of insight into how they would have dealt with it back in the old days. They'd have bad days where they'd be taking some shit off their boss and briefly picture everybody in the office hacked to bits, or find themselves idly speculating on how they could use their kid's Meccano to build a death-less robot ninja. Every time they got too close to the truth, gas would fill the room and they'd wake up, giving it hip-hip-hooray at a family birthday party. It was a kind of metaphor for frustrated human potential, and its own potential was well and truly frustrated when *The Incredibles* came out later that year.

I had an idea that one of the super-villains would be Dark-seid. He'd have got picked up unconscious after failing to extinguish the sun or something, and to the FBI he wouldn't be this immense cosmic force, he'd just be another guy in tights who'd get his head wiped and go have a job in the sub-urbs. I imagined his wife coming home one day to find that he'd been hosing the whole garden with a flamethrower, with just charred ash remaining.

Do you like it honey?

I pictured him going to group therapy, trying to open up.

I want to destroy all life and replace it with anti-life. Does that make me a bad person?

I suppose I think that not only does blindly following sci-ence have a religious element, the counter-movement that says science is a religion is *even more* religious. With ideas of constant progress and man's higher purpose from one side, and singularities and leaps of consciousness from the other, it all smells like church to me.

Religion permeates everything. Atheism has always seemed deeply silly to me. 'Atheism' comes from the word 'theism', so it's already defined by religion. You might as well say you are a Satanist. Not much harm ever came from someone believing things, except the occasional time when a guy believed that his hands were talons and a hitchhiker was his mother. The real trouble comes when you decide that other people have to believe. How is the idea of a leap in consciousness different from that? 'Everybody needs to join me, everything they think is wrong.' We're so surrounded by religion that even the ways we think to escape it are religious. Maybe atheists were created by God to bore us into accepting his love.

I wish for a world in which the concept of religion doesn't even exist. I think this is finite, your life, that's all there is. That the human experience is finite, that everything will die, that there will be complete heat death of the universe and then nothing. It's a hard thing to accept but when you do it makes every moment so much more vital to enjoy. I think it would be better to forget our civilised attempts to process death and embrace the brutal reality. I think people should accept death more, even the ultimate death of everything. Is that just my bleak religion? Or does that mean I just want to program everybody with the anti-life equation? *I want to destroy all life and replace it with anti-life. Does that make me a bad person?*

The pope stepped down. It meant a billion Catholics were temporarily leaderless, unsure exactly why they should hate themselves. Benedict talked of turbulent winds and rough seas. He was obviously speaking figuratively: by turbulent winds he meant child-abuse scandals, and by rough seas he meant child-abuse scandals. He left St Peter's with the words that he was now just a simple pilgrim, before being flown by helicopter to his cliff-top castle. Many criticised Benedict's anti-condom stance, but I suspect he just thought that if more kids are born HIV positive it might make priests a bit less inclined to shag them. I confess I'm no expert when it comes to popes, but surely the best one's still Tom Baker.

When it came, the smoke from the papal conclave was created by a unique blend of fivers, witness statements and DNA evidence. As is traditional, Cardinal Bergoglio changed his name when he became pope. A tradition that dates back to when CRB checks began. Pope Francis was chosen to become the first ever South American pope, as they've got a history of shooting children rather than, well, you know.

The new pope always used to take the bus instead of a limo. Why? Well, would you want to turn up at your mistress's house in a limo that has Church plates? Here's my modernisation tip, if he wants it. Dips for those communion crackers. He's going to try to improve the Catholic Church's image, surely the religious equivalent of shampooing Ernst Stavro Blofeld's cat. Buenos Aires's priests love spending time in the slums. Well, if you think not many people take notice of kids, imagine how few bother listening to poor ones.

OK. Here's a theory. Just a theory. After he's elected, the new pope goes to that room in the Vatican and reads their biggest secret. It's not priests that are horny for kids, it's God that possesses the priests. Earth is nothing more than a sex farm for a malevolent, paedophile God. That's what the pope compartmentalises that night. Why does Satan possess children? To make them spew bile; to be unattractive to the paedophile God. Satan is the good guy in all of this.

Or maybe it simply read:

Jesus came to us with an important message of hope. By his life he taught us that one in twelve people is a cunt. Fewer than you'd think. With Jesus dead for three days, Satan re-made the world in his image. Jesus ascended to heaven, defeated. Happy Easter.

A lot of people have been asking me what I think about celibacy for priests? I think it would be a good idea. A scrap of parchment unearthed by scholars suggests Jesus might have taken a wife. I doubt it. If he were married and disappeared for three days he wouldn't have dared to come back.

There were rumours a priest in the Vatican was caught watching transsexual films just last year, although it turned out that the man in the dress was just a reflection in the screen. The Vatican is keen to stamp this practice out or else priests' urges could be so greatly reduced they'll no longer bother turning up for choir practice.

Web firm TorrentFreak has revealed that computers in the Vatican have been used to download porn films. I suppose that explains why the former pope always had to hold on to someone as he walked. Perhaps a little more tolerance of bondage in religion would be a good thing. After all, the Middle East would be a much more tranquil place now if Moses hadn't been so uptight and vanilla about Pharaoh being so into the whole master/slave thing. It's sobering to think that if only the Egyptian leader had been into a different fetish fundamentalist Jews might nowadays break bread on the Sabbath not in skullcaps and ringlet sideburns, but in naughty-nurse outfits.

Ultra-Orthodox Jewish men can now buy glasses with lenses that only let them see clearly for a few metres, thereby reducing the risk of viewing immodestly dressed women. I worry there's a slight flaw to the plan. Ten thousand years of alcohol use would tend to suggest that girls being out of focus doesn't make men less inclined to want to shag them. Surely it's better to see attractive women when they're at a distance; if they suddenly just emerge from the fug you've much less time to disguise a semi.

And farewell Reverend Moon, the cult leader who amassing an eye-watering fortune while demanding total obedience from followers. Followers could come nearer to God by having sex with Moon himself. I hear that although the process could cleanse your soul, he'd usually end up making a right mess of your tits. He built a business empire that included media chains and arms factories, and lived in a palace while his followers lived frugal lives. Amazing to think that someone like that was the head of a religion, and not a political leader.

• • •

The Church of England voted against women bishops. An outrage, as those old cathedrals can get so dusty. But it's understandable that women bishops weren't allowed. I mean, 80 per cent of a bishop's job is map reading, unscrewing the lids off jars and disposing of spiders. Opponents argue that this issue is a lot more complicated than it seems and they *certainly* don't have time to explain it to a load of women.

I've done everything I can to campaign for women in the Church. Whenever I play chess I insist on making tiny breasts from Blu Tac and attaching them to my bishops. Why not let women become bishops? If I'm to be told a fairy story I'd prefer it to come from someone who looks like my mum.

The Church of England then signalled its opposition to gay marriage by taking a 550,000-signature petition to Downing Street, although I must say I don't know if it's really appropriate to protest against sodomy by shoving such a big document through a poor wee letterbox.

Scotland, however, went ahead and introduced gay marriage. We've never had anything against gay people in Scotland. Unless by gay, you mean English. Cardinal Keith O'Brien said that proposals to legalise gay marriage were 'grotesque'. Actually, it makes perfect sense for homosexuals to marry each other as they're the only group of men that don't actually hate going to weddings. The cardinal accused the government of trying to 'redefine reality'. This from someone who worships a magical man living in the clouds. Of course, Catholics insist that a man should not lie with another man. I'm guessing that's what's led to their 'under-fourteen' loophole. To be honest, when it comes to same-sex matters like this I always reach for my trusty Bible. It's just the right thickness so that when I kneel on it Ricardo can more easily get his **** in my ****.

And then, of course, Cardinal Keith O'Brien was accused of 'acting inappropriately'. I heard he played a sordid trick on a blind bell ringer. Just imagine it. The young priest finishing his night prayers. The cardinal's voice. 'You'd better hope he was listening.' Then the unmistakable rasp of a zip.

Why is everyone getting so wound up about this? They're saying gays want to marry in church, not bum each other in the vestry. What are churchgoers worried about? Do they think that they'll kneel down to pray and someone will stick their dick in their mouth? But there's nowhere gayer than church – there's loads of blokes wearing frocks, pictures of a half-naked man on the wall who they say they love, and they won't allow women to join in. The Church of England has to realise that everyone has to keep up with progress. I mean, look at me – my VHS of *Footloose* isn't worn out but it's not stopped me updating to LaserDisc. Jesus would have been a great gay man – with those extra holes in his hands and feet he'd have been all sorts of fun. Lady Gaga says the pope's opinion on gay marriage 'does not matter to the world'. Most people don't care about the opinions of a man in a silly outfit. But, sadly, millions do still care about what the pope has to say.

Jeremy Irons has claimed gay marriage could be used as a way to avoid inheritance tax if a son married his father. This is the latest in a long line of strange statements from Jeremy. It seems like every time he opens his mouth he ends up putting his dad's cock in it. Sorry, I meant foot. It's this bloody permissive society that's warping my mind. I can't even think bent. I mean straight. Jeremy is possibly unhappy about gay marriage and he finds the best way to distract himself from the thought of two adult men agreeing to a loving relationship is to block it out by picturing himself shagging his own dad. I guess we all have different ways of dealing with stressful situations.

Lord Tebbit raised the same point about this. His son must be devastated that his dad only wants to marry him for his own money. Tebbit made his anti-gay comments in an interview with homeless newspaper *The Big Issue*, a publication he actually helped start – by being part of Margaret Thatcher's cabinet. I suspect his dislike exists at a deeper level. He may have seen gay men stripped to the waist and glistening with sweat, and subconsciously thought they might be mining coal. Tebbit insists he doesn't necessarily object to seeing a gay couple together at the altar, so long as it's in boxes following a shame-induced suicide pact. Tebbit raised the possibility of a lesbian queen. She'd be a lot like the normal queen, but with fewer corgis and more cats. In private, Tebbit apparently confesses he'd be happy to attend a gay church wedding. He could cover then his body in gold paint in order to leap down from the crucifix at the crucial moment and shout, 'Not on my watch, ladymen!'

The bill to make same-sex marriages legal was passed in parliament. Lesbians will now be allowed to marry – so if I were you I'd invest heavily in companies that make white dungarees. There's too many innuendos involved in weddings – you don't want to ask, 'Who's going to play the organ?' and have half the congregation shout back, 'Buy us a drink first, love.'

I only have two reservations about gay marriage. First, it's against the holy teachings of our Lord. Second, it could fundamentally undermine ratios at wife-swapping parties. Of course, the official Catholic position is against. As opposed to the unofficial Catholic position, bent over the font biting down hard on a hymn book.

Plans for gay marriage have been approved by MPs despite opposition from nearly half the Tory party. They're worried their rent boys will propose. One chief opponent is Tory MP Peter Bone. A little rich, as I'm sure I saw his name on the credits of *Dishonourable Members 2*. I won't go into details, but let's just say afterwards they had to take a nailbrush to the Mace.

It's astounding that in 2013 there's still currency in hinting at people's sexual preferences. So, to help this practice wither in the bright light of public exposure, I'm going to reveal my own. I'm happy to admit I like being filmed being mounted by a giant screeching eagle with a four-metre wingspan. There, I've said it.

ENDGAME

My premise is that our society is now completely subsumed by advertising and that the roots of our unhappiness lie in our attempts to market ourselves and live the advertised life. The original PR bible, the foundation of modern marketing and politics, is called *Propaganda*. It was an attempt to use the ideas of Freud to influence opinion and was written by Freud's nephew, Edward Bernays.

It's not just that we're being marketed to or marketing ourselves, it's that this is all being done in a Freudian framework. I've always felt ambivalent about psychoanalysis. I've thought of going into therapy, but I know it'd be like hiring a window cleaner for a burning building. Also, I can't help feeling that perhaps the first question you should ask your psychiatrist is why you're such a cunt that you have to pay someone to listen to you.

I mean, I like Freud, but a culture in which dreams are interpreted as communications from a deeper self would sit pretty easily in a fantasy novel. And underneath is the idea of the primacy of sexual urges. The culture thinks that all you're interested in is pussy.* Happy pussy, sexy pussy, loving pussy, warm, forgiving pussy. That's what motivates you. Friendly pussy, plain pussy, available pussy, your friend's pussy – you don't care. Depressed pussy, drunken pussy, angry pussy, stripping out by the airport pussy, ugly pussy, hospital pussy, dead pussy. Is this base view of humanity, right through the wiring of our society, part of the reason our society can treat people as if they're so base?

I wonder if a more useful idea for understanding reality might be James Joyce's notion that we're trying to live within the stories we tell each other as if they're real. Do you ever try to look objectively at your own life as a narrative? Do you ever see yourself as the bad guy in the story? Hey, don't judge me, I'm forty and I do whatever I have to do to get a hard-on together. Modern life is the struggle to awake from narrative. We now have stories fed to us from birth till death, and because they used to be a survival mechanism we take them too seriously. Stories will originally have been about *little boys who left caves when they heard noises*, and we still give them that kind of weight.

Were men of my dad's generation emotionally withdrawn because of John Wayne and Gary Cooper, or vice versa? I remember as a teenager thinking that in a good relationship you had to have these funny arguments all the time. That's what you saw in films and on TV. And, really, they only put conflict in stories so it's easier to write dialogue. What would

* Female heterosexuals and male homosexuals should here read 'pussy' as 'cock'.

Batman and Green Arrow talk about if they were getting along? *I like your boots, motherfucker.*

My five-year-old boy has a favourite American teen sitcom, and after an episode he'll spend an hour speaking out of the side of his mouth, trying for their brand of 'tude, and not making any sense. And it's fun. It's fun getting zinged by someone who I could probably convince that the moon is a gobstopper.

But your life is not a story, your consciousness is not a narrator. It's a godless, authorless world.

In addition, you get other people trying to 'lay their trip on you'. I love that phrase, an old acidhead shorthand for having someone try to tell you how to view the world, or yourself. The thing that middle-class critics and comics always praise in working-class comedians is self-loathing; acts producing characters or jokes where the real targets are themselves. This seems to be a quality never demanded of middle-class comedians; indeed, they generally seem quite pleased with themselves! The uncomfortable question of why they want to see their social inferiors hate themselves never really seems to come up. Like Malcolm X before me,* I never bought that self-hate bullshit. I don't hate myself any more than I love myself. I'm a rich, sex-haunted, world-class nutcase who will probably die horribly. You go deal with it.

We're brought up in a language and a culture. It's like a prison we're born into. If you're a kid right now, you're already negotiating a world filled with sexuality and violence

* It feels great to write that phrase down. Try it!

and emptied of ideas. You must wonder why people sing in their pants, why your dad can't look at you with the same intensity as at his smartphone. You won't wonder when people started preferring work to life, when they became more concerned about how they seem than what they are – it'll just be how things have always been, and the bars of your prison will be narrower than those of your parents.

Language is a key part of your prison. Taboos over language are often just a childish attempt to draw a circle round all the good people. I run into people every day who use all sorts of language that would be unacceptable on stage, but does this make them immoral? Language taboos change regularly and these people don't get the updates, they don't read broadsheets, they don't watch documentaries and, perhaps most importantly, they don't really care how society thinks they should talk. So is the taboo value of a word like, say, *retard*, really always about morality or ablism? It's obviously also a handy way of recognising social class. This is before we even get to the fact that things have different meanings for different people. You say snapchat, I say speedwank.

I remember some nutter at a party one time telling me about his idea that jihadis would welcome a nuclear war. That they longed for the United States to turn the world into a desert, because jihadis would flourish in the desert, and it's all part of the plan for a successful Armageddon. If the Americans blast the world into sand they'll have created the very terrain where they'll be defeated. I actually think that's a pretty useful metaphor for where we're at culturally. Let me explain.

There's an episode of Graham Norton that I enjoy so much I watch it regularly. It's playing now in the background as I write this. It features a bizarre central performance from Gerard Butler, who speaks in an alarming drawl and maintains an excited and distracted manner throughout.

It starts with Graham Norton dressed as one of the warriors from *300* shouting 'This is Sparta!' and announcing the guests in a cod Scottish accent. Because they've got Butler on the writers will have sat there and thought of various *300*-themed intros. The way this works in my experience is that writers produce things of various levels of wit and complexity, which the producers fret their way though, worrying about whether they're obvious enough for the punters on BBC One. I mean, would they have had to have seen the film for this joke to work? Do you think people might just wonder why Graham is dressed as a Greek warrior this week, that maybe he's going to do the interviews like that, perhaps adopting a classical mindset, leading to a list of questions being asked that sound outlandish to our modern ears? In the end the producers will have gone, 'Fuck it. Let's just have him shout "This is Sparta!" and just announce the guests in a Scottish voice.' It's a moment of such artistic poverty that it's made me question the pointlessness of creativity and mankind's impossible battle to communicate. I'd go so far as to say that it constitutes an important coda to the theory of evolution.

The guests are Butler, Martin Freeman and Amy Pond from *Dr Who*, who enter one after the other with a real frisson of tension, as if Butler had tried to finger everybody in the green room. This is quite a common set-up for the Graham Norton couch, where one alpha male flirts with an attractive woman, while a less potent man looks on, stricken.

What follows is a shifting and uneasy dreamscape that can be seen as a satire on the nature of celebrity, a chilling expressionist commentary on how we can never truly communicate, and even just a show that was knocked together with a kind of bored contempt for the human mind.

Butler lunges at an anecdote about a kilt but claims never to have worn one. A fan in the audience shouts out that he wore one to a première that Tuesday. Butler's eyes swivel with the amazed wonder of a time traveller. He then attempts an anecdote about surfing that falls a little flat. Norton shrieks, 'Not exactly comedy gold!', idly dismissing this little tidbit of Butler's life that's offered up to him, like some mischievous sprite from a lost Shakespeare play.

There's a heavy, musky sense of sexual threat throughout. Amy Pond looks both excited and frightened, and would clearly bolt if she were a horse. Martin Freeman wears a mask of acceptance that he's to be overshadowed both professionally and sexually. It's a mask that questions how appalling Butler would have to be to lose the admiration of the crowd or the girl, that says even a sudden shift into a spasmodically delivered murder confession might not be quite enough.

Then somewhere, somehow, a complex helmet that boosts the wearer's psychic abilities must have been handed to the young William Burroughs, because it transpires that the little Jack Russell from the film *The Artist* is to make an appearance, re-enacting Butler's surfing anecdote to thunderous applause.

We have to weave our own dramas around shows like this simply because to take them as they are meant would be too harrowing. This is the kind of imagination that our dead culture has forced on us. Like a kung fu monk, held by his enemies at the bottom of an old well, we use the power of our minds to create a paradise of rolling hills, peopled by imaginary families, having imaginary kung fu themed adventures in our starless prison.

So, we're in a cultural desert. The great TV and cinema and public intellectuals that I grew up with have been blasted into sand. What qualities there are in our culture now are just the mirages we project on to great piles of nothing. But what's culture, anyway? Culture is simply a machine designed to get you to think within certain fixed parameters. Culture isn't your buddy. Your culture is a series of products designed to advance the status or wealth of a stranger, and anyone who it hasn't caused to completely give in to despair by their late twenties is just shallow.

Everything produced in culture nowadays has a minimal impact because of the increasing speed of information. Let's say you can write a TV drama and succeed in producing something interesting in the face of all the practical problems and restrictions. I don't think you can, but let's imagine that you do. Fewer people than ever before will watch it, and when they do they'll be texting, tweeting, watching a five-second mpeg of someone masturbating onto a photograph of Vanessa Hudgens. It has taken me about an hour to write this paragraph because that sentence made me go and look at nude photos of Vanessa Hudgens. Modern life is really only about learning the bare minimum you need to know about a subject to have an argument. You can write a bestselling book but half the people who buy it won't read it and the ones that do won't finish it. A lot of your prospective audience is now on prescription medication. With an increasing demand for never-ending content, we all plagiarise and parody ourselves.

So give it up. Stop trying to do something for posterity, because posterity doesn't exist anymore. Stop living for tomorrow, because there's really no guarantee of that, either. Yes, you live in the discarded carapace of a dead civilisation, but you can turn it into the beautiful life of an apocalypse survivor. Enough good books and films have been made that you can watch or read something mind-blowing every day until you die. You can thrive like a jihadi in the desert of our culture. Show me the most intellectual nihilist and I'll show you someone who's simply ignoring a lot of really good reggae.

If you're truly wise you'll see ahead of you days of war and nights of love. Yes, you're stalked by corporations, but they're just monsters. Monsters are things you learn how to kill – they have weaknesses and obey the rules of stories. And, as you fight, put aside your differences. However much your comrade annoys you, rest assured that these beasts are going to have the same serial number for your world-view in their camps. Make a break from a world of hate crimes without returning to one where we let people die through sheer fucking indifference.

And the key to happiness? I don't know. Meet someone beautiful who's aroused by failure? Really, it's to escape your own ego, not just on a personal but on a political level. We live in a society of elitism and exceptionalism, and it has seeped into all of us. Bombing civilians is an attempt to export democracy. Civilians fighting back are terrorists. What's OK for us is not OK for you. Pussy Riot are the victims of tyranny, but not the people we jail for throwing a custard pie at Rupert Murdoch or swimming in front of the Boat Race? They were actually doing something selfless, however foolish, and we can't have that. The self has to be before you at every turn, every sentence that's spoken weighed up for its impact on your status, every person you meet reduced from incredible possibility to a very poor mirror.

The self is just an excuse to pour endlessly into a leaky bucket. Why not focus on your real mirror, your children? I was in the swimming pool the other day and as I floated listlessly in a corner I suddenly realised that I wouldn't do comedy again, that the day I'd have needed to start warming up for a new tour had long gone and I hadn't even noticed.

My boy was on one of his periodic anti-social highs. So, I'd grab him, imprison him in a hug and whisper this deliberately boring story in his ear in a low, doleful Irish voice that was a partial satire on his grandad. 'The Story of the 100 Sheep,' I began, listing all the different places a forsaken sheep would go looking for a friend. 'He looked in the hills and he looked in the meadow and he looked down by the stream. And he didn't see any sheep. Then he looked in a hedge and he saw a sheep. Then there were two sheep! The two sheep were lonely and decided to go looking for a friend . . . They looked in the hills . . .'

When it got to about five sheep, a few of them got lost in the fog and it was back to two sheep. Then one sheep sat down to begin telling the other 'The Story of the Thousand Crabs'. As the laughter shook him, it rose through me like music.

ALSO BY FRANKIE BOYLE:

'Boyle has made his name with the kind of acerbic comedy that takes no prisoners and leaves those of a timid disposition gaping, slack-jawed.'

Independent